Seeds of the Spirit

SEEDS

of the Spirit

WISDOM OF THE TWENTIETH CENTURY

Edited by

RICHARD H. BELL
with
BARBARA L. BATTIN

with an
Introduction by Richard H. Bell

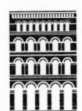

WESTMINSTER JOHN KNOX PRESS
Louisville, Kentucky

*We dedicate this book to
Barbara L. Bell, Richard's wife,
whose strength and courage in this past year
have been an inspiration;
and to
John Buzza, Doug Loving, and Barbara Troxell,
who have been graceful guides
and dear companions on Barbara Battin's journey.*

Book design by Publishers' WorkGroup
Cover design by Vicki Masden Arrowood

Cover: *The Gleaners,* Jean-François Millet (French, 1814–1875), etching, 7⅞ x 10⅛ inches; from the John Taylor Arms Print Collection. Gift of Ward and Mariam C. Canaday, 68.73. Courtesy of The College of Wooster Art Museum, Wooster, Ohio. Used by permission.

First edition
Published by Westminster John Knox Press
Louisville, Kentucky

This book is printed on acid-free paper that meets the American National Standards Institute Z39.48 standard. ∞

PRINTED IN THE UNITED STATES OF AMERICA.

95 96 97 98 99 00 01 02 03 04 — 10 9 8 7 6 5 4 3 2 1

Library of Congress Cataloging-in-Publication Data

Seeds of the Spirit: wisdom of the twentieth century / Richard H. Bell, Barbara L. Battin. — 1st ed.
    p.   cm.
  Includes bibliographical references.
  ISBN 0-664-25465-9 (alk. paper)
  1. Spiritual life—Christianity. 2. Spiritual life—Judaism. I. Bell, Richard H. II. Battin, Barbara L.
  BV4501.2.G574   1995
  291.4'4—dc20
                                             94-48631

Contents

Preface

When Cynthia Thompson, then of Westminster John Knox Press, asked me to do this book, I looked around my office library and realized that scores of spiritual classics on the shelves were well worn and had given me strength of spirit on many occasions. So the task did not appear too daunting. I thought it would be one of reacquaintance with some old friends and joyous explorations with some new spiritual sojourners.

What soon became obvious was the difficulty in deciding what to include and what to exclude; where were spiritual boundaries to be drawn? How could the word "classics" apply when dealing with contemporary authors? What criteria would be inclusive enough without risking diffusion of focus? There were no easy answers to these and more questions. What finally emerged is a result of reflecting on about thirty years of selective reading in the vast sea of the literature of Western "spirituality"; listening to friends for whom this literature likewise has had value; and making a few rather arbitrary decisions that concluded, "She's in, he's out." Why is one writer in and another out? Often because the twentieth-century spiritual landscape could not be traversed without including obvious writers, such as Thomas Merton, Teilhard de Chardin, Dietrich Bonhoeffer, Dag Hammarskjöld, Evelyn Underhill, and Abraham Heschel, while many less familiar writers of our century, I concluded, simply had to be introduced to a larger public—writers such as Lanza del Vasto, Maggie Ross, Alexander Schmemann, Simone Weil, Joseph B. Soloveitchik, Václav Havel, Catherine de Hueck Doherty, and a Carthusian monk.

So these gleanings are a sampling tested in conversations with wise colleagues and friends, adding a bit here and taking away a little there—always finally satisfied that the selections would please others as much as they continually did us in our compiling. Barbara Battin had eyes for passages I might not have seen, and unexpected suggestions came from Don Saliers, Kathleen Norris, Joseph Kaippayil, and Maggie Ross. To them I am especially grateful. Barbara has contributed by sharing in the gleaning and in writing Appendix A, "Some Practical Uses of Gleanings for Spiritual Reading and Spiritual Formation." She also made many helpful suggestions and revisions to the Introduction.

Meg Braun, a student at The College of Wooster, worked with me during the summer of 1993 through our Sophomore Scholars Program in compiling information for the biographical sketches and even took a hand in gleaning from a favorite author of hers, C. S. Lewis, as well as from Catherine de Hueck Doherty. Meg's good humor and hard work has been deeply appreciated.

Throughout the summer of 1993, my family went with little or no vacation but continued to support my work. Barbara Bell, my spouse, in the midst of her own work and preparations for her Library Fellows' assignment to Namibia, often read drafts of material and kept her spirits up through personal hard times. Her strength has been an inspiration to me, and to her I lovingly dedicate this book.

Amy White, secretary to the departments of philosophy and geology at The College of Wooster, offered significant technical assistance in the preparation of the manuscript. With great appreciation, her help is gratefully acknowledged.

Cynthia Thompson, at Westminster John Knox Press, seemed to know when to lean on me in finding the right audience and when to trust my judgment. Thank you, Cynthia.

In most instances, only a few passages were gleaned from any one book of an author, but with a number of books there were greater harvests to pick from, and permission to quote extended passages was sought. In a few instances, tracking down permissions has proved nearly impossible. We have, however, noted all sources and will gladly correct, in a subsequent printing, any omissions we may have made.

Richard H. Bell
Barbara L. Battin

The College of Wooster
May 5, 1994

Acknowledgments

We are grateful to publishers and copyright holders for permission to use excerpts from the following:

Daniel Berrigan, *Sorrow Built a Bridge: Friendship and AIDS;* Baltimore, Md.: Fortkamp, 1989 (1-800-43PEACE/1-800-437-3223).

Dietrich Bonhoeffer, *Life Together;* English translation copyright © 1954 by Harper & Brothers, copyright renewed 1982 by Helen S. Doberstein. Reprinted by permission of HarperCollins Publishers, Inc.

Dom Helder Camara, *Hoping against All Hope;* Maryknoll, N.Y.: Orbis Books, 1984. Used by permission of Orbis Books; Claretian Communications, Inc., Quezon City, Philippines; and HarperCollins Publishers, Blackburn, Australia.

Dom Helder Camara, *Em Tuos Mãos, Senhor! (Into Your Hands, Lord),* PAULUS, Rua Francisco Cruz 229, 04117-091 São Paulo—SP, Brasil.

A Carthusian, *The Way of Silent Love.* Used by permission of Cistercian Publications, Kalamazoo, Michigan, and Darton Longman & Todd, London.

Catherine de Hueck Doherty, *Poustina: Christian Spirituality of the East for Western Man;* Glasgow: Fontana Books, 1977. Used by permission of Ave Maria Press, Notre Dame, Indiana.

Dag Hammarskjöld, *Markings,* translated by W. H. Auden and Leif Sjöberg. Translation copyright © 1964 by Alfred A. Knopf, Inc., and Faber and Faber Ltd. Reprinted by permission of Alfred A. Knopf, Inc., and Faber and Faber Ltd.

Abraham Joshua Heschel, *God in Search of Man,* copyright © 1955 by Abraham Joshua Heschel and renewed © 1983 by Sylvia Heschel. Reprinted by permission of Farrar, Straus, & Giroux, Inc.

Nancy Mairs, *Ordinary Time,* copyright © 1993 by Nancy Mairs. Reprinted by permission of Beacon Press.

Thomas Merton, *Contemplation in a World of Action;* New York: Image Books, 1973. Permission granted by the Merton Legacy Trust.

Henri Nouwen, *The Life of the Beloved;* New York: Crossroad, 1992. Reprinted by permission of Crossroad.

Flannery O'Connor, *The Habit of Being,* edited by Sally Fitzgerald. Copyright © 1979 by Regina O'Connor. Reprinted by permission of Farrar, Straus, & Giroux, Inc.

Franz Rosenzweig: His Life and Thought, by N. N. Glatzer, copyright © 1953 by Schocken Books, Inc. Reprinted by permission of Schocken Books, published by Pantheon Books, a division of Random House, Inc.

Mother Teresa, *A Gift for God,* copyright © 1975 by Mother Teresa Missionaries of Charity. Reprinted by permission of HarperCollins Publishers, Inc., and HarperCollins Publishers Ltd.

Mother Teresa, *The Love of Christ,* copyright © 1992 by Harper-Collins Publishers, Inc. Reprinted by permission of HarperCollins Publishers, Inc.

Seeds of the Spirit

The word "glean" means to gather together good grain (or other material) after a reaper. In Bible times, when the harvest had been laid away, those in need would enter the fields and glean here and there. We have come after and gleaned here and there from the greater harvests of some of the best-known and best-loved spiritual writings of the twentieth century.

We are, in some ways, like Ruth, who gleaned from fields that were not in her own country. She entered new and foreign fields.[1] The result of her gleaning in these new fields was most fortunate. Boaz took notice of Ruth and was kind to this foreigner (Ruth 2:10). She found a new home, a new family, and a new faith. In their mutual encounter, Boaz and Ruth created "new life," which provided a link into the future for their whole community (Ruth 4:14–15).

We have entered many new and foreign fields and gleaned these passages to offer the reader a companion for spiritual growth. In doing so, we invite further reflection and action on a wide range of issues, as the twilight hours of our troubled twentieth century pass toward the dawning of hope in a new century. The harvests from which we glean are all from the twentieth century; they are from persons who spoke with a sense of prophecy to their particular time and who speak with wisdom to all or any time and its human needs.

The wisdom gleaned is from several spiritual traditions within the Christian and Jewish faiths, though some lie on the margins of these. We come to this task from the Protestant tradition, and our lives have been deepened over the years by our exposure to the richness of this literature, which cuts across faith boundaries. To keep the focus clear, we have limited our selections to works from the American and greater European traditions. All our gleanings speak in a universal and unified voice to our time.

We have three goals in presenting these gleanings to our readers:

1. that the gleanings will aid in personal spiritual growth and inspire the hearts of all who read them with attention;
2. that they will be used to spark renewal in community building within congregations, and also to encourage discussion of personal faith development within one's own tradition;
3. finally, that they will be useful, particularly to those searching for greater religious challenge in their lives, by encouraging a spiritual reading of scripture and by fostering further reading and reflection in the rich tradition of spiritual writings. In these ways they may be of special assistance to pastors in preparation for preaching.

Each set of gleanings has parallel scripture passages; there are brief biographical sketches of the authors from whom we have gleaned; and there is a selected bibliography of mostly recent works on spirituality for further reading. Throughout this book we have used inclusive language. We have, however, not altered the language in the "gleanings" themselves.

What may be called spirituality is always reflected in human lives. It comes through the witness of men and women in our world. Such witness often finds its way into words, and these words can be like seeds for us. We must turn and till the soil of our ordinary lives and plant these seeds in our hearts and minds. There they can be given life and grow in everyday practice. Our task in this book is to provide some seeds of the spirit that come from the century into which all of our readers were born.

WHAT IS SPIRITUALITY?

The spiritual life is like a dance with a partner who has a fertile imagination and who leads. We must be alert, responsive to the slightest in-

2

dication of his intention, supple, ready to adapt to the movements with which he woos us.

—A Carthusian

Spirituality is like a dance where we must learn to follow the lead of the sacred in our lives. It is a pathway on which human beings travel and find themselves at home with God in this world. As a "religious" way of being, spirituality evokes how the sacred breaks into the ordinary of human life.

The concept of spirituality is directly derived from the biblical concept of *ruach* or "breath," the "breath of God over creation," and is linked closely to the Holy Spirit. Lawyer and theologian William Stringfellow placed spirituality clearly in its biblical context when he said, "Biblically, the Holy Spirit means the . . . presence of the Word of God inhering in the life of the whole of creation."[2] The Holy Spirit is the Holy Word at work renewing the integrity of life in this world. At the heart of biblical spirituality is attentiveness to the presence of God's Spirit, which renews life as whole and holy.

Spirituality means "living in the spirit" and refers to the quality of spiritual presence we can receive into our lives. That sense of presence is linked to various forms of grace and to our human acts. Paul, in his letter to the Galatians, referred to such acts as "works of the Spirit"—among which he listed purity of heart, patience, perseverance, self-control, love, joy, gentleness, kindness, and peace (Gal. 5:22–23). Faith and works of the Spirit go hand in hand (James 2:14–16). What we call spirituality relates to how we live in this Spirit and how we pursue a greater intimacy with the presence of God. Living in the Spirit is finding ways to allow God's Spirit to break gracefully into our lives.

Spirituality is finding our feet on unstable ground, changing unrest to rest, turbulence to calm, violence to love, war to peace; it means being witness to the incarnational presence of God wherever we discern God's absence.

There is, however, a certain clutter and ambiguity surrounding the frequent use of the term "spirituality" that must be addressed. Today, "spirituality" is often linked with "new age" ideas and activities or with the occult—with physical-culture activities such as dietary regimens and jogging, with cults and mind control, or with crystals and alternative healing remedies. It has associations with such religious extremes as total abstinence, wilderness sojourns, stigmata, and fasting, to mention but a few.[3] We will try to avoid these fringe meanings and stick closely to a biblical and historical use of spirituality.

At the heart of the Jewish and Christian traditions, spirituality refers to the most profound of human struggles, where human weakness meets the silent God, and where the horizons beyond our human ability to know are calling men and women to reach beyond themselves. This tradition becomes increasingly clear as we discuss the concept of spirituality through its major Jewish and Christian exponents in this century and as we glean from their writings.

Love of Neighbor

Spirituality is fundamentally a matter of ethics, of how each person lives toward another person in this world. Ethical actions, in the words of Jewish writer Emmanuel Levinas, are not what prepare us to meet God; rather, they are the very way in which God enters our world and illuminates it. Spirituality is present through the love of God as shown in acts of love toward our neighbor. Abraham Heschel, America's premier Jewish theologian of this century, says that Jewish spirituality understands God "by sensing the living acts of God's concern" and by seeing that "God's goodness is . . . a specific act of compassion" (Heschel, 21). This emphasis on acts of love of neighbor is not only true of Jewish spiritual writers. The Christian tradition, as we shall see, also focuses on individual acts of compassion as the way through which God enters the world.

All religions converge on this point in spirituality, and it is through spirituality that humans transcend sectarian boundaries. Thus, if our different theologies are often characterized by their doctrinal *divergence*, a spiritually based theology would be characterized by its *convergence* of God with the human world.

In a very Christ-centered remark, the French spiritual writer Simone Weil says that the gospel reveals that the one "who gives from true compassion gives Christ himself." Humans should be present in the world through compassion. "Compassion is the visible presence of God here below. . . . Compassion . . . is the rainbow," she says. What a marvelous image—a rainbow linking God's love to us through

4

our compassion to others. This love is the human enactment of a sacrament. It is God's act of creation, incarnation, and consecration, bringing into this world on the arc of a rainbow the love of God that lies at the other end.

Silence and Warmth

In the midst of World War II, Simone Weil wrote that what human beings need most "is silence and warmth; what [they are] given is an icy pandemonium." Our greed, excessive competition, and frantically paced life have created this "pandemonium." And it turns "icy" when you add to these various crises the alienation that so many continue to feel because of faceless technologies, materialistic greed, and the bureaucracies that have numbed our lives. Consider the many young, well-educated, and able men and women today who feel especially alienated with the offer of nothing better than menial work (what has come to be called a "McJob").

Simone Weil's image of "icy pandemonium" evokes our sense of isolation and aloneness, our unconnectedness, and the burden we have of "making it on our own" in an inhospitable world. This condition shaped the spiritual writings of our century.

What does Simone Weil (among others) mean by our need for "silence and warmth"? Silence recalls the spirit. It allows for a period when the pandemonium in our lives can be collected, bracketed, put aside. It affords the possibility of thinking about absolutely nothing, a refreshing change from a mind-filling busyness. Silence allows time to look into one's self and to give attention to the world around the self. It allows time to consider the face of an Other. Attention is one of the great by-products of silence. We gain an increased ability to see aspects of our world that we have passed over. We become more alert and sensitive to human need—our own and others' needs. Silence is a gift that we seldom share or give to others. It is a difficult and most desired possession that we seem to have lost the capacity to exercise. That is perhaps why Simone Weil says that it is one of our greatest needs. The importance of silence for spirituality becomes evident in our gleanings.

Warmth as a need has two sides. First, we all want to have a home, a place where we will be nourished and respected as a whole person. Warmth signals wholeness, so that we can carry on the ordinary affairs of human life without a sense of being splintered or fractured. It means having sufficient food and shelter so that we have the energy to hope.

Second, warmth implies compassion. When we have enough warmth, we can give to others and also can receive from others without fear or threat of being used or abused. With warmth comes trust. The "icy" part of our pandemonium melts away when such trust enables us to follow our more creative passions, knowing that others will attend to different basic needs that we can then share. Then our creativity can become a gift to others. In this sense, warmth is a foundation stone for community.

Spirituality, then, requires silence and warmth, both of which are aspects of the splendor of this universe. Consider the silence of the heavens and the mysteriousness of all living things, the fragility of our ecosystem and the need to care for one another and for the living world that surrounds us. Silence and warmth put us in touch with these larger things and thus with the living Spirit and the spirit of living.

Spirituality is that part of theology's center that shows us that seeking is finding God and that loving one's neighbor is the way of bringing God to light in our world. The seeds of such seeking and loving in the Jewish and Christian traditions go back very far, and the history of spirituality reaches deeply into the Hebrew and Greek scriptures. Not only is a tradition of spirituality a deeply embedded part of the sacred texts, but it has historically passed through Judaism in varying forms, such as the talmudic tradition, the Cabala, and the traditions of Hasidism. It has passed through Christianity in the early desert wisdom, the medieval mystical traditions, and certain strains of Protestant pietism.

But what about a legacy of spiritual writers from the twentieth century? How do they continue a tradition of spirituality that is particularly relevant for the turn of the millennium and for safer passage into the twenty-first century? If some of these writers were responding to the tyranny of two world wars, the nuclear peril, the rise of greed, and the arrogance of power, how can they guide our spiritual journey beyond such obstacles? How can they help us find greater silence and warmth, feel at home in our strange land, and give new hope for our children and grandchildren?

At present, many people are looking for a meaningful life in a world that seems to have abandoned God. God, however, has not abandoned humankind, and as long as there are humans who seek God and show compassion to one another, God will be found in our midst.

As we move into the twenty-first century, we need a theology that is responsive to a postnuclear, post-Holocaust, secular environment where we are a wandering and seeking people. Spirituality as understood in this book, we believe, can provide an ordinary "religious" philosophy to guide individuals along the increasingly thorny paths that we call our human life; it can be the root and branch for a new theology of the twenty-first century.

THREE DIRECTIONAL GUIDELINES
IN TWENTIETH-CENTURY SPIRITUALITY

Three directional guidelines can be traced through major twentieth-century spiritual writers. We will see how these writers kept faith both with their sacred traditions and with the whole thrust of "spirituality" as we have introduced it. These guidelines are: Jewish spirituality, Christian incarnational spirituality, and natural spirituality.

In many ways, these three directional guidelines provide a map for understanding the many gleanings. As we draw this map, we will introduce a small sampling of gleanings to show the richness of the fields from which they have been gleaned. The gleanings reflect the fire in the hearts of their authors and hold up new light and warmth for all to receive.

Jewish Spirituality

Abraham Heschel defines the term *spiritual* as follows:

> This is what we mean by the term *spiritual:* It is the reference to the transcendent in our own existence, the direction of the Here toward the Beyond. It is the ecstatic force that stirs all our goals, . . . turning arrivals into new pilgrimages, new farings forth. The spiritual is . . . something we may share in. . . . When we perceive it, it is as if our mind were gliding for a while with an eternal current.

As we move toward the next millennium, there are very clear directional tones sounded among twentieth-century Jewish writers that point toward a spiritually centered theology. These directions are not well understood, especially by non-Jews. Our gleanings come from several writers: Martin Buber, Abraham Joshua Heschel, Emmanuel Levinas, Franz Rosenzweig, and Joseph B. Soloveitchik. These writers guide us in three directions important for understanding Jewish spirituality. We are guided, first, toward seeing God as revealed in and through our deeds; second, toward recognizing the importance of the sacred text (toward a strong biblical spirituality); and third, toward understanding the importance of community and memory.

Sacred deeds. Heschel writes, "If God were a theory, the study of theology would be the way to understand Him. But God is alive and in need of love and worship." A living God in need of love and worship squarely places the responsibility for being a spiritual person on deeds, on love and compassion, and on justice and gratitude in worship. This emphasis on the living God, and hence on our lived response, is why Jewish spirituality is said to be principally "ethical." Key to Franz Rosenzweig's spirituality earlier in the century was what he called "the offensive idea of revelation" (Rosenzweig, 31). He called it "offensive" because it pointed to the divine breaking into the lowly, human sphere. By our deeds we become reflections of God's presence in the world. Heschel sums this up nicely: "Our task is to bring God back into the world, into our lives. To worship is to expand the presence of God in the world. To have faith in God is to reveal what is concealed."

Living, worshiping, and being faithful show God's presence in the world. What ordinary people *do* is the pathway for revealing God. Three trails lead to God, says Heschel: "The first is the way of sensing the presence of God in the world, in things; the second is the way of sensing [God's] presence in the Bible; the third is the way of sensing [God's] presence in sacred deeds." With such sacred deeds must go a willing heart—a "joyfulness" and "gladness of heart" (Deut. 28:47; 6:5–6; Ps. 100:2; Prov. 3:17–18) directed toward love of God and neighbor. This willing directedness is what is called in Jewish tradition *kavanah,* or "the art of setting a deed to inner music," or "intoning" God into our hearts.

It is a distortion of Judaism to say it is a religion of the law, if what is meant is that it is legalistic. The legal side of Judaism (what is called the Halakhah) is empty without moral teachings (or Haggadah), and both the law and the moral teachings must come together as one song in the heart (*kavanah*). "*Kavanah*," says Heschel, "is the same as attentiveness . . . attentiveness to God" and not to a "text" or "law" or "doctrine" (Heschel, 314–15).

For both Martin Buber and Emmanuel Levinas, true Jewish spirituality always involves a "threesome": "I," "you," and God (or the self, the "other," and God). It is in our meeting and being responsible to our neighbor that the face of God is shown on this earth. For Buber, a genuine human dialogue transforms the other person from an impersonal object to a "Thou." God's great dialogue with humankind is played out in our particular conversations with one another. Levinas says the response to the love of God for humanity "is the love of my neighbor." "The justice rendered to the Other, my neighbor, gives me an unsurpassable proximity to God."

Sacred texts. Building on themes of our human struggles in this world and our desire to find God in the dialogues of our life, Joseph B. Soloveitchik, a rabbi who has influenced many (especially in America), returns us to the concept of the Halakhah, the law of Torah (rules for living based on the Torah). He sees it as a covenantal framework; for him, the law as lived out in the heart is the sunrise and the sunset between which every day is a blessing. Soloveitchik says that the person who lives the law in this way—one whom he calls a "halakhic" person—"craves to bring down the divine presence and holiness into the midst of space and time, into the midst of finite, earthly existence." These remarks capture the essence of Jewish spirituality, living in the here and now, with a consciousness of divine creation as the reason for my love of neighbor. It is a concrete spirituality that is directed toward this world, bringing God into intimate dialogue with human life. The covenantal framework is found in living through the sacred texts.

A Jewish spirituality also emphasizes the Bible as the revelation of God; it is the Holy Book that "sanctifies life." What the Bible does, says Heschel, is to "scatter seeds of justice and compassion, to echo God's cry to the world and to pierce [our] armor of callousness." It is also in the Bible that order in our life is sanctified in the Sabbath, in a meal, in daily prayers, and in holy days and liturgy. These are important ordering and redeeming activities for Jewish spirituality. They are of equal value to ethical acts and to the law. They sanctify the deeds. Reading the Bible and living its sacred practices—keeping traditions of worship active through the community—these are a life source of Jewish identity.

Community and memory. Finally, Jewish spirituality places great emphasis on the community and its memory. There is a "covenantal faith community" among men and women. Community is shaped in adversity and struggle through common practices around a sacred center. When such community is alive, God goes forward through it and the continuity of the revelation and tradition are maintained. Rosenzweig, a mentor to virtually all Jewish writers of this century, emphasized the community as a place of conversation where the Hebrew scriptures and prayer are central—scriptures "must guarantee the connection between the center and the periphery of the community."

One of the most important opportunities for community in both Buber and Rosenzweig is the family meal. It begins for Rosenzweig with "silent listening"—and thus the possibility of hearing. "The common meal with its silent community represents actual community alive in the midst of life." Buber says, "There is no better symbol of communal life than the banquet." He understands the communal meal as a holy altar. In the whole pattern of ritual practices, Jewish spirituality both reveals the sacred in daily life and also builds community through memory as it moves toward redemption.

Christian Incarnational Spirituality

Karl Barth stands as the most towering Protestant theologian of the twentieth century and, arguably, as the theologian from among all traditions of the West who has contributed most to the reformulation of Christology, that is, of restoring the central place of Jesus Christ in understanding human reality. This latter in particular, as we shall see, is crucial to sustaining a spiritually based theology within the Christian faith. It has not been easy for any Protestant theologian to use the traditional language of Christian spirituality through what have been called the many "crises of humanism"—

crises that have grown from human arrogance and power as seen in two world wars, the rise of fascism and totalitarianism, and forty years of cold war hostilities. The language of spirituality was thought to be the province of Catholic and Orthodox theologians, or of mystics and marginal religious movements. This does not mean, however, that Protestant Christianity, along with other Christian traditions, has lacked a spiritual center. Our gleanings from Karl Barth, Dietrich Bonhoeffer, C. S. Lewis, William Stringfellow, and Maggie Ross show how deeply rooted their work is in the notion of God present to us in Jesus Christ. This incarnational fact is the shared center of all Christian spirituality.

Immanuel. Karl Barth calls his view of the incarnation "God's humanism." This particular relationship between God and humanity, where God enters into the actual life of a human being, is, for Barth, an experience of "God's loving kindness." In all of Barth's vast writings, he focuses on the gospel as "the good news of God's presence and work in Jesus Christ." Because of God's presence and work in Jesus Christ and Jesus' own humanity, Barth also says that "the gospel is centrally concerned with humanity." There is, as in Jewish spirituality, a strong ethical message here that focuses on love of one's neighbor: "Human being," says Barth, "is being with other humans" (Barth 6, 6). With Barth, however, as with all Christian spiritual writers, our very love of neighbor, our being with other humans is made possible through the redeeming grace of God *as God reveals God's self in the world*. Grace means Immanuel—God with us.

In one short sentence, Southern writer Flannery O'Connor captures the spirit of this incarnational spirituality: "You will have found Christ when you are concerned with other people's sufferings and not your own."

Our "being human" is conditioned by the particular incarnational act. In this act, God transformed the world so that humans can realize their love in and through the person and spirit of this unique human being, Jesus of Nazareth, historically and spiritually "emblazoned" in creation. Because God enters creation in the form of a human being, humans can turn their work and all of creation toward the love of God. There is a single movement involving the coming forth of God to humanity and the return of humanity to God. Our love, because of Jesus and the Spirit that he bequeathed to us, is a "new" love, as revealed in a "new" testament of God's love for us.

The "insinuating" Christ. Much of incarnational spirituality is not so "theologically" or "dogmatically" formulated as Karl Barth often made it sound. The "two natures" of Jesus, the God-Human, are seen more often in the literature of Christian spiritual writers as constituting an animating, transforming, and sanctifying agent that courses through creation and into which human life must weave itself, creating new patterns of being. These new patterns of being, guided by the incarnate Jesus and God's Spirit, are the heart of what Christians mean when they say they are new beings in Christ. As Thomas Merton says, the meaning of the New Testament faith is "that all life, all truth, all hope, all reality may be sought and found 'in Christ' " (cf. Phil. 3:7–11). Faith is realized in life as one conforms one's self to the life of Christ, or "takes on the Christ." Merton believes that Christ is a dynamic principle within our soul.

The papal encyclical *Mater et Magistra,* by John XXIII, expresses this "Christ dynamic" well by saying that our human work is a continuation of "Jesus the Divine Redeemer's" work; as we "take on" Christ, Christ's power is transferred by what is called *kenosis.* Kenotic theory has to do with God's self-emptying and self-giving in Christ, which in turn can be participated in by ordinary humans emptying themselves of their egos so that Christ can unite with them. This view is also reflected in the gleanings of Maggie Ross and the Carthusian.

In a more poetic mode, we find an almost mystical expression of this dynamic in these words of the famous scientist-priest Pierre Teilhard de Chardin: *"in Christo Jesu"* is "a certain quantity of spiritual power" that "insinuates itself everywhere and is everywhere at work"; and elsewhere, Christ is "a center of radiation." Finally, Teilhard says, "The immense enchantment of the divine *milieu* owes all its value in the long run to the human-divine contact which was revealed at the Epiphany of Jesus."

At the center of most Christian incarnational spirituality connected with this Christ-centered dynamic are the concepts of attention, renunciation, love, and peace.[4] We will only briefly remind the reader here of these points, as they are taken up at length in the gleanings. In an early spiritual writing of this century, Evelyn Underhill said that when you "look with the eyes of love," you create an attitude of "receptiveness" and "surrender your I-hood." This is a form of attention and renunciation, of considering another face to face. It is an emptying of one's self when the self is viewed as sufficient and independent of the need of God and help from others. Such attention and renunciation, says Simone Weil in her essay "Human Personality," put us in touch with the "impersonal" of the other and create the possibility of an "unconditional love." This is a love not dependent on some personal return or on the other's attractiveness or wealth or wit. It is a love that transpires simply because the other is recognized as a human being.

One of our most exalted tasks is described by Pope John XXIII: "Every believer in this world of ours must be a spark of light, a center of love, a vivifying leaven amidst his fellowmen: and he will be this all the more perfectly the more closely he lives in communion with God and in the intimacy of his own soul. In fact, there can be no peace between men unless there is peace within each one of them, unless, that is, each one builds up within himself the order wished by God."

The love, compassion, and peace that follow through God's incarnation in Christ and from such human attention and renunciation as we can cultivate are best summarized by the first letter of John, where we are reminded that Christ "laid down his life for us—and we ought to lay down our lives for one another." We must be like "little children," abiding in Jesus Christ and Christ abiding in us. All this is done by "the Spirit that he has given us" (1 John 3:16–20, 23–24).

Descending images. It is in the Russian and Greek Orthodox Christian traditions, however, that an incarnational spirituality is most dramatically expressed. With the birth, death, and resurrection of Jesus, God's transformation of the world is complete. Our world is already made sacred, and it is our human task to discern Christ in the world and to live joyfully in Christ's life. Happiness is not found in the world. Happiness is in the joy of life that has broken into the world, and we must "enter into" this joy! The great joy is that the Lord is present in the world. Russian Orthodox priest Alexander Schmemann says, "A Christian is the one who, wherever he looks, finds Christ and rejoices in Him. And this joy *transforms* all his human plans and programs, decisions and actions, making all his mission the sacrament of the world's return to Him who is the life of the world." This Schmemann calls a "sacramental vision" of human life—a turning of our concrete, everyday lives into a living sacrament that participates fully in Immanuel—God having come down to us.

Earlier in the twentieth century, another Orthodox theologian, Pavel Florensky, gave us a different way of thinking about the incarnation through his discussion of the meaning of an icon, or sacred painting, which depicts God's grace through a human figure. His notion of the icon as a "descending image" beautifully captures the essence of Eastern Christian incarnational spirituality. An icon is a "descending image," he says, "a product of light," proceeding from the light of God. Descending images are "a sign of the Holy Spirit," whose presence is concrete and visual. They are an incarnation of the divine essence through the material world. These are contrasted by Florensky with "ascending images," which are characteristically found in Western art.[5]

The whole notion of God's light descending into and through an icon—as experienced in, for example, *The Holy Trinity*, by Russia's greatest icon painter, Andrei Rublev; in a Duccio madonna and child; and to some degree, in one of El Greco's monks—is a wonderful metaphor for incarnational spirituality, where God's revelation is decidedly *with us*, in this world and life, and not "beyond." God comes through, for example, the tilted head of the Mother of God casting divine light on the Holy Child, which passes on directly to the viewer. We are thus brought into communion with God. Such *communion* with God, rather than a *mystical union* (the goal of some advanced holy men and women), is the most desired end of all forms of spirituality. It is an end accessible with God's grace meeting our human desire in attention and love.

Natural Spirituality

Much of twentieth-century Christian theology had a way of closing the door on God for many people. If no attention is given to the spiritual side of its theologians' writings, then much of Christianity's popular image becomes austere. The more prophetic traditions of Protestantism suffered from this loss of the spiritual. Let us venture a brief answer to the question: Why did so many people turn away from traditional theologies and from the church in our century, especially in Western cultures?

Within the Lutheran and Reformed traditions (and other mainline denominations), God often seemed lofty, and ordinary human beings were diminished. To be fair, in context this development was a response to human triumphalism—our arrogance of power—and this theology served to call us back to God's sovereignty and to remind us of our creatureliness. Nevertheless, with all our growing "independence," an increasing number of people saw no need to return to such a remote God, and besides, God had not come to the rescue of the millions of afflicted persons in the world. To many, especially in Europe, a "godless" response to life seemed as hopeful as a "godly" one. The existentialist writer Albert Camus was as inspiring for carrying on life's tasks in the face of what seemed absurd as was the church. Many young people also felt alienated from the practices of the church, finding it oppressive and forgetful as it failed to listen and respond to our century's upheavals.

The liberal theologians held out hope that humans might be good by their own will and overcome the troubles of the age. But if we could, by our own moral mobility, overcome our numerous crises, then why would we need God at all? God, understood in liberal theology as merely "my co-pilot," lost out to the efficiency syndrome that one could take control of the aircraft oneself just as well. Liberal theology ends with the "death of God."

Fundamentalism became an alternative for some, but it often has not fit well into the general direction and spirit of our age. It appears reactionary to our scientific habits and "modern" sensibilities, often rigid to new openings for women and minorities, intolerant of human diversity and the new pluralisms, and economically hostile to ecologically urgent initiatives (not to mention its frequent dogmatic tendencies). A perceived lack of openness has been an obstacle for many.

Hunger and hope. It is sad to say that by the last quarter of the twentieth century much of the theological landscape was drying up. Humans, however, still have not lost their hunger for God or their will for meaning or their hope that the human race is worth caring for.

They believe they can still manage their fair earth and have a capacity for love and mutual trust for one another deeply seated within. With this hunger, will, and hope, there is a new spiritual direction opening for us; there is a way forward that appeals to those who have fallen away from mainline theologies, who have seen no point to liberalism, and who cannot fall back to fundamentalism. It is also a way that has a great appeal to the young, to those born in the last third of the twentieth century, who did not live through some of the century's major "crises" or feel moved by the century's dominant theologies. This we call a *more natural spirituality*, one that tries to discern the sacred in the ordinariness of our human life. Let us turn now and sketch out several aspects of this new spiritual direction.

In mid-century, the Roman Catholic Church moved to reform itself through its Second Vatican Council. This was invigorating for millions of dispossessed and powerless people, especially in Latin America and Africa; it gave new impetus to a fledgling liberation theology. Vatican II made possible the local development of faith and Bible study, and an indigenous liturgy became more accessible to ordinary people. Unsuspectingly, it unleashed a wave of hope and a new way for simple human beings to turn toward God, to praise God in their own tongue, and to empower themselves within their local communities. In retrospect, Pope John XXIII unleashed a whirlwind of the Spirit that still whispers hope around the globe.

One of the movements of change brought about by this unleashing of the whirlwind was that of Creation Spirituality. Dominican priest Matthew Fox drew on some of the medieval mystics such as Julian of Norwich, Mechtild of Magdeburg, and especially fellow Dominican Meister Eckhart, as well as later "mystics" such as Pierre Teilhard de Chardin. Drawing on these writers, he suggested a reversal of the starting point for theological reflection and for spiritual experience of God. Instead of beginning with original sin as the definitive point for the journey of life and spirit, Fox spoke of "original blessing." His emphasis was the goodness of creation, the goodness of our embodiment as human beings, the goodness of both our sexuality and our spirituality. This Creation Spirituality seeks to heal the ancient divisions between nature and spirit, the world and God. It understands the cosmos itself to be a rich source of revelation of

God's intention for all of creation. It links prayer with politics, spiritual practice with the pursuit of justice for the earth and its people.

Fox took traditional Christian spiritual disciplines and practices and contemporized them. He added what he called a "creative way" and a "transforming way" to his Creation Spirituality. He renewed old rituals and developed new ones, using as a resource the wisdom of native peoples and incorporating their love and ethical values related to the earth. Fox's most recent contribution is his work on the "Cosmic Christ," the manifestation of divine/human authentic humanity, of which Jesus Christ was the model and in which those who follow him find their full vocation. The Creation Spirituality movement, though it had its inception in the Catholic Church, has spread well beyond its bounds and has an ecumenical appeal for those seeking alternatives to the established churches of many religious traditions.

"Monastic witness." Growing out of the incarnational direction of spirituality is another pointer for a new spirituality—one embedded in what William Stringfellow called a new "monastic witness" (Stringfellow 3, 81). Poet and essayist Kathleen Norris says of such a monastic witness that it is "a way of surrendering to reduced circumstances in a manner that enhances the whole person. It is a radical way of knowing exactly who, what, and where you are, in defiance of those powerful forces in society—alcohol, drugs, television, shopping malls, motels—that aim to make us forget."[6] "To be a monk," she says, "means being still and at peace, at home in mind and body and at ease with one's place."[7] Thomas Merton similarly says of his own monastic witness that he finds ways to love his brothers and sisters through deeper solitude and silence.

This new monastic witness is a spirituality without the trappings of doctrinal language. It tries to glimpse "the Word behind the words," where the Word may be a nameless silence. It is a spirituality that arises from human experience, which reflects on life as being more than matter. It witnesses to our desire not to live alone and our will to share our lives with and to care for others. It is a spirituality that has drawn tens of thousands of young people from every continent to monastic communities such as Taizé in France, where silence and simple words and deeds spur renewal and send persons away with hope and new convictions about their meaningful place in the world.

One of the primary virtues of this new spiritual direction is its call to us to *stop*—not to act as if we always have to get somewhere. It asks us to *look* into our neighbor's face, to *listen* to the cries of those who are hurting, to *feel* at one with our natural earth. This is an attitude of *attention* to being and surrender to the moment in which we live. It focuses on the importance of contemplation and action as two sides of the same coin. This point rings clear in the gleanings from Simone Weil, Dag Hammarskjöld, Brother Roger, and Lanza del Vasto, among others. Again, Kathleen Norris writes, "We are seeking the tribal, anything with strong communal values and traditions. But all too often we're trying to do it on our own, as individuals. That *is* the tradition of middle-class America, a belief in individual accomplishment so strong that it favors exploitation over stewardship, mobility over stability."[8]

Journeys to wholeness. This aspect of a new spirituality is also focused in women's spirituality. Here love, accord, joy, care, and birth are significant themes in how we can best experience a sense of the Spirit in the world. Writer Carol Ochs calls such spirituality a way of *knowing through being*. She says that spirituality is a "coming into relationship with reality." It "is fostered not by studying the lives of mystics but by increasing our knowledge-through-being by living our own lives as authentically as possible."[9] Spirituality, in this women's perspective, involves a "profound commitment of loving" modeled after "the female maturational process that emphasizes nurturing—coming into relationship."[10] "In the course of loving we feel pain, loss, abandonment. And in the course of loving we see reality and value transforming the world."[11] An interesting feature of Ochs's conception of spirituality, which grows out of women's experience of mothering, is that it goes against the "journey metaphor" prevalent in traditional Western spirituality. "Women's experience in mothering," Ochs says, "places value in the *process*, not in the final goal."[12] The journey is understood *as* home!

Women's spirituality stresses journey as end, not as means. Here again, the point is that of lived experience, of loving in the present. It is relational with the natural world and with other human beings, not individualistic and goal-oriented. This remark gleaned from Nancy Mairs in *Ordinary Time* summarizes this perspective: "God is here. And here, and here, and here. Not an immutable entity detached from time but a continual calling and coming into being. Not transcendence, that orgy of self-alienation beloved of the fathers, but immanence: God working out Godself in every thing. Process, yes, that's what I want to explore and celebrate, the holy as verb, Godding, not Godness or Godhood. What she does. How she does it" (Mairs, 11).

The sacred in the secular. There are two generations of people in central and eastern Europe and in China who had God ideologically wrested away from them by communism in the twentieth century (after World War II). And in the Soviet Union for seventy years (from 1920 to 1990), God was little more than a shadow confined to a conceding Russian Orthodoxy, to a church all but dead apart from its Divine Liturgy, which was an extraordinary example of God's Spirit present in time. But in spite of these systematic assaults on organized religion, a form of spirituality survived. There was an unflagging human spirit giving presence to a sense of the sacred, which found ways to live beyond the repression. This spirituality turned inward toward the resources of the human spirit. It found that silent hope could live on in the midst of social lies. It recovered the power of freedom bestowed by some mysteriously transcendent source through its own condition of powerlessness. Now that the external walls of these repressive regimes have crumbled around the world, that spirit (this new form of spirituality) is finding new voices.

Among those voices is Václav Havel, shepherd of the "velvet revolution" in Czechoslovakia and president of the Czech Republic. In 1984, just out of prison, Havel wrote, "We must not be ashamed that we are capable of love, friendship, solidarity, sympathy and tolerance, but just the opposite; we must set these fundamental dimensions of our humanity free from their 'private' exile and accept them as the only genuine starting point of meaningful human community." These "fundamental dimensions of our humanity" do not arise in a vacuum; they find their origins in a preexisting sense of the sacred. This sense of the sacred is, for Havel and others, "the natural world," which bears within it "the absolute which grounds, delimits, animates, and directs it." Sometimes Havel calls this absolute God, while at other times it is just the "absolute horizon" or transcendent spirit. Whatever it is called, without such an absolute Havel believes we are plunged into a spiritual and moral crisis. It is humanity's task to restore the spirit and find ways to reanimate love, friendship, solidarity, tolerance, and community in life itself. He said in a letter to his wife from prison in 1980: "Ever since childhood, I have felt that I would not be myself—a human being—if I did not live in a permanent and manifold tension with this 'horizon' of mine, the source of meaning and hope" (Havel, 1, 101).

Havel's spirituality is perhaps best characterized as a "natural spirituality," living in the tension between the "absolute horizon" and everyday "concrete horizons," through which we must act truthfully toward our brothers and sisters and toward the natural order that our technology has so profaned.

Havel, like Levinas, who influenced his thinking, says that "face-to-face with . . . [our] neighbor," we experience a primordial sense of responsibility. This experience is so fundamental that it radically changes human relationships. It creates conditions for "human communality." Again, writing to Olga, he repeats his litany of ways to relate "face to face" and shows how such relating can transform our world. "Love, charity, sympathy, tolerance, understanding, self-control, solidarity, friendship, feelings of belonging, the acceptance of concrete responsibility for those close to one . . . [are what] . . . shape the fate of the world." These activities are "life-giving." They renew the human spirit and become signs of hope.

This is a profound form of spirituality that builds on the Jewish and Christian traditions but recognizes the new reality that has abandoned God and ceded responsibility over to purely utilitarian ends. Havel and others wish vigorously to deny this secular reality that has abandoned God in favor of one that affirms our responsibility within a sacred framework. Havel finds signs of hope—though often "timid"—in many things: "in genuine peace movements, in varied activities in defense of human rights, in ecological initiatives, in short, in all the constantly recurring attempts to create authentic and meaningful communities that rebel against a world in crisis" (Havel, 1, 372).[13]

Community and holiness. Finally, there is one aspect of this new direction of spirituality that requires a brief word before we begin our gleanings. This aspect of spirituality places emphasis on the reanimation of tradition and on the building of community—an emphasis not totally missing from any of our directional guides.

The focus on community can be seen in the development of what are called "base communities" in Latin American religious life, especially in the way in which many Catholic parishes have restructured their local religious life around Bible study and local concerns. In base communities, traditions are renewed and local problems are analyzed with an eye toward communal solidarity and social change. It is also revealing that in North America the growth of "house churches" has been phenomenal in the past decade. Mutual dependencies and sharing, modeled after the first-century church (Acts 2:44–47), are at the heart of this development. It is also worth noting that holiness and a sense of community are reflected in the "new monasticism" thriving around the globe.

Greater emphasis on reciprocity is also a part of ecology movements, where we recognize the fragile structure of human and biological communities and our need for greater cooperation and mutual care. In their concern for the earth, humans are coming to understand themselves as part of a larger living cycle of things and, furthermore, that all living things are sacred. This new understanding needs to be celebrated, and such celebrations are in themselves spiritual acts. Through celebration, the sacred surfaces in the ordinary course of our lives.

The very notion of community embraces the reality that each thing relates to every other thing, that one's human choices affect another's world. When natural turbulence happens beneath the sea or breaks through the earth's surface, this changes the ground on which we stand and the air we breathe. When plants, insects, and humans die and new life emerges, the whole world is altered. This holistic and connected way of seeing and understanding our human-earthly life points to community and reciprocity, and these call out for a new spiritual communion.

Our century has specialized in abandoning tradition and thus separating humans one from another. Such abandonment unravels the narrative threads of family and community and leaves "individuals" to create their own destinies. A sacred or holy dimension of life could be restored if persons could find "new ways of interpreting and refashioning a local tradition in order to bring into being a new, universal order to replace the contemporary disorder."[14] We in Western society, atomized and separated one from another as we are, would do well to rediscover something like a sense of community as "holy rite" or as passage from individualism to a shared common act. This sense of community—through a meal, a simple greeting, a shared neighborly act, a revival of a few local traditions, new respect for the earth, authentic participation in some "secular" ceremony or divine liturgy—can reanimate the holy in our life.

CONCLUDING REMARKS

The convergence and commonality of all these twentieth-century spiritual writers can be woven around the theme of how God or the sacred becomes manifest in the world *as* human beings show love to one another. Divine love has made our love possible, and our loving is the sign of that divine love. There are different ways of construing the Divine, but its presence is obviously a dynamic and living presence in the world. In these senses, what is common to twentieth-century spirituality is sacred presence in nature, as incarnation, and through community and compassion within the human family.

In twentieth-century spiritual writings there is a focus on the concrete—the here and now, the eternal in time—and on the urgency of humanity reclaiming its roots in some sacred center, so that the "warp speed" of our lives does not send us swirling toward breaking point. If humans can hold the center with forms of caring for one another, we will be gathering the peace of the Spirit into our midst and will be witness to a new dawn. We will be offering new hope for our children and their children's generations. In these gleanings are seeds for searching and stretching one's own life and for many forms of caring; they are evidence that we have "drawn God down" in our search for meaning and have given to life, and to love itself, a quality of holiness.

Who are the twentieth-century writers from whom we glean these passages? The following list is not exhaustive of interesting writers on spirituality but it represents the best within the traditions we have discussed. These writers are women and men who have made an important difference in their particular time and place through their personal witness and their writings: Hans Urs von Balthasar, Karl Barth, Daniel Berrigan, Anthony Bloom, Dietrich Bonhoeffer, Martin Buber, Dom Helder Camara, a Carthusian monk (of Grand Chartreuse Abbey), Dorothy Day, Lanza del Vasto, Catherine de Hueck Doherty, Matthew Fox, Gustavo Gutiérrez, Dag Hammarskjöld, Václav Havel, Abraham Heschel, Pope John XXIII, Martin Luther King Jr., Madeleine L'Engle, Emmanuel Levinas, C. S. Lewis, Nancy Mairs, Thomas Merton, Henri Nouwen, Flannery O'Connor, Karl Rahner, Brother Roger of Taizé, Franz Rosenzweig, Maggie Ross, Alexander Schmemann, Dorothee Soelle, Joseph B. Soloveitchik, William Stringfellow, Pierre Teilhard de Chardin, Mother Teresa of Calcutta, Evelyn Underhill, and Simone Weil.

Note: In the "Gleanings" section that follows, the citation at the end of each passage refers to its *author,* the *text* from which it is taken, and the *page number* in that text. Texts are listed by number under author in the "Biographical and Bibliographical Essay" at the end of this book. For example: *Daniel Berrigan* (4, 171) refers to Daniel Berrigan's *Sorrow Built a Bridge,* page 171.

The wisdom of these authors is organized under headings that have been historically and personally central to the traditions of spirituality. Some authors' gleanings cluster around only one or two spiritual themes, while those of other authors have something to say of significance to many themes. All are there as seeds of the spirit to engage us in new and challenging conversations about our own sense of the sacred in our ordinary lives; all can direct us to the partner in the dance that is the spiritual life. Let the dance begin.

Gleanings

The Gleaners, Jean-François Millet (French, 1814–1875), etching,
7⁹⁄₁₆ x 10¹⁄₁₆ inches; from the John Taylor Arms Print Collection.
Gift of Ward and Mariam C. Canaday, 68.73. Courtesy of The College
of Wooster Art Museum, Wooster, Ohio. Used by permission.

GLEANINGS

Alienation and Loneliness

We have in common a terrible loneliness. Day after day a question goes up desperately in our minds: Are we *alone* in the wilderness of the self, alone in this silent universe, of which we are a part, and in which we feel at the same time like strangers?

Abraham Heschel (101)

Pray that your loneliness may spur you into finding something to live for, great enough to die for.

Dag Hammarskjöld (85)

Today, after being bemused for several centuries with pride in technical achievement, we have forgotten the existence of a divine order of the universe. We do not realize that labour, art and science are only different ways of entering into contact with it.

Simone Weil (4, 168)

He who attempts to act and do things for others or for the world without deepening his own self-understanding, freedom, integrity and capacity to love, will not have anything to give others. He will communicate to them nothing but the contagion of his own obsessions, his aggressiveness, his ego-centered ambitions, his delusions about ends and means, his doctrinaire prejudices and ideas. . . . We have more power at our disposal today than we have ever had, and yet we are more alien-

27

ated and estranged from the inner ground of meaning and of love than we have ever been. The result of this is evident. We are living through the greatest crisis in the history of man; and this crisis is centered precisely in the country that has made a fetish out of action and has lost (or perhaps never had) the sense of contemplation. Far from being irrelevant, prayer, meditation and contemplation are of the utmost importance in America today.

Thomas Merton (4, 178–79)

At its best our age is an age of searchers and discoverers, and at its worst, an age that has domesticated despair and learned to live with it happily.

Flannery O'Connor (2, 159)

This, then, is our desert: to live facing despair, but not to consent.

Thomas Merton (9, 22–23)

The essential characteristic of the first half of the twentieth century is the growing weakness, and almost the disappearance, of the idea of value.

Simone Weil (5, 167)

The race to succeed, to get ahead at all costs: what devastation this is for Christians! When someone has no other means of regaining confidence in himself, he is doomed to dislocation, he empties away the best of himself.

Brother Roger (3, 142)

The world itself is in danger of being plowed open, from a place of teeming life to a cosmic grave. The world itself is grown Lazarine, the human race is rolled in a shroud.

Daniel Berrigan (2, 116)

A nation that continues year after year to spend more money on military defense than on programs of social uplift is approaching spiritual death.

Martin Luther King Jr. (1, 9)

In the face of death, live humanly. In the middle of chaos, celebrate the Word. Amidst babel, I repeat, speak the truth. Confront the noise and verbiage and falsehood of death with the truth and potency and efficacy of the Word of God. Know the Word, teach the Word, nurture the Word, preach the Word, defend the Word, incarnate the Word, do the Word, live the Word. And more than that, in the Word of God, expose death and all death's works and wiles, rebuke lies, cast out demons, exorcise, cleanse the possessed, raise those who are dead in mind and conscience.

William Stringfellow (1, 142–43)

We note with dismay the purveying of death, at home and in the world; not just physical death, which in comparison with other forms and disguises is indeed a far lesser evil. But I think of that "second death" of which the Bible speaks; a spirit of death that freezes the soul; death of the heart, numbing of the mind, death to compassion, to a sense of the truth, to a sense of one another. And worse; the "putting to death," with malign intent and sour will, of human variety, of sexual and racial and religious variety, all that "wet and wildness" celebrated by the poet, to the honor of the Creator.

Daniel Berrigan (4, 230)

If anything sets apart our 20th century from all previous centuries—fundamentally and not just on the surface—then above all it is the extreme sharpening of two opposing, antithetical understandings of human life and of man himself. One view affirms that man is man precisely because of the spiritual thirst within him, a searching, a restlessness for transcendence. For the other, man begins his human destiny only after having killed this thirst.

Alexander Schmemann (1, 12)

To walk according to the Spirit is to reject death (selfishness, contempt for others, covetousness, idolatry) and choose life (love, peace, justice). To renounce the flesh and live according to the Spirit is to be at the service of God and others.

Gustavo Gutiérrez (2, 70)

The life of Jesus has made it very clear to us that the spiritual life does not allow by-passes. By-passing loneliness, hostility or illusion will never lead us to solitude, hospitality and prayer.

Henri Nouwen (8, 11–12)

When you are forever fighting a degenerating sense of "nobodiness";— then you will understand why we find it difficult to wait. There comes a time when the cup of endurance runs over, and men are no longer willing to be plunged into an abyss of injustice where they experience the bleakness of corroding despair. I hope, sirs, you can understand our legitimate and unavoidable impatience.

Martin Luther King Jr. (2, 6)

People have a very acute appreciation of the price they have paid for outward peace and quiet: the permanent *humiliation of their human dignity.* . . . The man who can resist humiliation can quickly forget it; but the man who can long tolerate it must long remember it. In actual fact, then, nothing remains forgotten.

Václav Havel (2, 31)

The great objection brought against Christianity in our time . . . is the suspicion that our religion makes its followers *inhuman.*

Pierre Teilhard de Chardin (1, 68)

When Christ said: "I was hungry and you fed me," he didn't mean only the hunger for bread and for food; he also meant the hunger to be loved. Jesus himself experienced this loneliness. He came amongst his own and his own received him not, and it hurt him then and it has kept on hurting him. The same hunger, the same loneliness, the same having no one to be accepted by and to be loved and wanted by. Every human being in that case resembles Christ in his loneliness; and that is the hardest part, that's real hunger.

Mother Teresa of Calcutta (2, 30–31)

Actually we are touching Christ's body in the poor. In the poor it is the hungry Christ that we are feeding, it is the naked Christ that we are clothing, it is to the homeless Christ that we are giving shelter. It is not just hunger for bread or the need of the naked for clothes or of the homeless for a house made of bricks. Even the rich are hungry for love, for being cared for, for being wanted, for having someone to call their own.

Mother Teresa of Calcutta (2, 39)

The Bible is an answer to the supreme question: *what does God demand of us?* Yet the question has gone out of the world. God is portrayed as a mass of vagueness behind a veil of enigmas, and His voice has become alien to our minds, to our hearts, to our souls. We have learned to listen to every "I" except the "I" of God.

Abraham Heschel (168)

[A basic need of "modern man" is] liberation from his inordinate self-consciousness, his monumental self-awareness, his obsession with self-affirmation, so that he may enjoy the freedom from concern that goes with being simply what he is and accepting things as they are in order to work with them as he can.

Thomas Merton (10, 31)

All of us, East and West, face one fundamental task from which all else should follow. That task is one of resisting vigilantly, thoughtfully and attentively, but at the same time with total dedication, at every step and everywhere, the irrational momentum of anonymous, impersonal and inhuman power. . . . We must draw our standards from our natural world, heedless of ridicule, and reaffirm its denied validity. . . . We must not be ashamed that we are capable of love, friendship, solidarity, sympathy and tolerance, but just the opposite: we must set these fundamental dimensions of our humanity free from their "private" exile and accept them as the only genuine starting point of meaningful human community.

Václav Havel (2, 153–54)

We must see the need of having nonviolent gadflies to create the kind of tension in society that will help men rise from the dark depths of prejudice and racism to the majestic heights of understanding and brotherhood.

Martin Luther King Jr. (2, 5)

Whatever the progress in technology and economic life, there can be neither justice nor peace in the world, so long as men fail to realize how great is their dignity; for they have been created by God and are His children. . . . Separated from God, man becomes monstrous to himself and others. Consequently, mutual relationships between men absolutely require a right ordering of the human conscience in relation to God, the source of all truth, justice, and love.

Pope John XXIII (1, 68)

I suppose what bothers us so much about writing about the return of modern people to a sense of the Holy Spirit is that the religious sense seems to be bred out of them in the kind of society we've lived in since the 18th century. . . . There is no sense of the power of God that could produce the Incarnation and the Resurrection. They are all so busy explaining away the virgin birth and such things, reducing everything to human proportions that in time they lose even the sense of the human itself.

Flannery O'Connor (1, 299–300)

Try to find time to stay alone with yourself: shut the door and settle down in your room at a moment when you have nothing else to do. Say "I am now with myself", and just sit with yourself. After an amazingly short time you will most likely feel bored. This teaches us one very useful thing. It gives us insight into the fact that if after ten minutes of being alone with ourselves we feel like that, it is no wonder that others should feel equally bored!

Anthony Bloom (1, 67–68)

Anger is indeed one of the main obstacles of the spiritual life. Evagrius writes: "The state of prayer can be aptly described as a habitual state of imperturbable calm." The longer I am here, the more I sense how anger bars my way to God. Today I realized how, especially during work which I do not like much, my mind starts feeding upon hostile feelings. I experience negative feelings toward the one who gives the order, imagine that the people around me don't pay attention to my needs, and think that the work I am doing is not really necessary work but only there to give me something to do. The more my mind broods, the farther away from God and neighbor I move.

Henri Nouwen (1, 29–30)

Many volumes would be needed to pursue the spiritual damage done us, the destruction of right thinking, by the past thirty years of nuclear mischief. A sense of being correctly centered, of being at ease, at home, rightfully in place in the universe, of being at least potentially brothers and sisters under whatever skies—all this is ruthlessly disrupted. . . . Irritation is the mood of the times.

Daniel Berrigan (3, 10)

The great spiritual call of the Beloved Children of God is to pull their brokenness away from the shadow of the curse and put it under the light of the blessing. This is not as easy as it sounds. The powers of the darkness around us are strong, and our world finds it easier to manipulate self-rejecting people than self-accepting people. But when we keep listening attentively to the voice calling us the Beloved, it becomes possible to live our brokenness, not as a confirmation of our fear that we are worthless, but as an opportunity to purify and deepen the blessing that rests upon us.

Henri Nouwen (4, 79)

The strategy of the principalities and powers is to disconnect us, to cut us off from the memory of God. It is not hard to see how many of our busy actions and restless concerns seem to be disconnected, reminding us of nothing more than the disorder of our own orientation and commitment. When we no longer walk in the presence of the Lord, we cannot be living reminders of his divine presence in our lives. We then quickly become strangers in an alien land who have forgotten where we come from and where we are going. Then we are no longer the way to the experience of God, but rather *in* the way of the experience of God. Then, instead of walking in God's presence we start walking in a vicious circle, and pulling others into it.

Henri Nouwen (5, 29)

The conduct of the powerful is almost invariably a mockery of God. Nothing more is required, by way of fulfilling the biblical formula for idolatry, than that the rich be themselves, that is, neglect the poor, live off them, exploit their labor, underpay them, rob them of dignity and hope.

And this sublime, self-deluded charade usually goes on in the midst of the most persuasive cover-up imaginable.

The ultimate deception, of course, occurs in one's own soul, persuaded of the justice of manifest injustice.

Daniel Berrigan (3, 9)

Our individual as well as communal lives are so deeply molded by our worries about tomorrow that today hardly can be experienced.

Henri Nouwen (6, 26–27)

The things that we love tell us what we are.

Thomas Merton (9, 24)

In the cross of Christ God confronts the successful man with the sanctification of pain, sorrow, humility, failure, poverty, loneliness and despair.

Dietrich Bonhoeffer (2, 15)

Parallel Scripture Passages

John 14:18–27	Psalm 28:1–2
Matthew 6:25–34	Psalm 130
Psalm 29:1–11	Psalm 142
Psalm 139:1–18	Isaiah 30:18–26
Psalm 42	

Attention and Listening

To "look with the eyes of love" seems a vague and sentimental recommendation: yet the whole art of spiritual communion is summed in it, and exact and important results flow from this exercise.

The attitude which it involves is an attitude of complete humility and of receptiveness; without criticism, without clever analysis of the thing seen. When you look thus, you surrender your I-hood; see things at last as the artist does, for their sake, not for your own. The fundamental unity that is in you reaches out to the unity that is in them: and you achieve the "Simple Vision" of the poet and the mystic.

Evelyn Underhill (2, 82–83)

[Speech] lives by virtue of another's life, whether that other is the one who listens to a story, answers in the course of a dialogue, or joins in a chorus. . . . In actual conversation, something happens.

Franz Rosenzweig (199)

To listen to someone is to put oneself in his place while he is speaking. To put oneself in the place of someone whose soul is corroded by affliction, or in near danger of it, is to annihilate oneself. It is more difficult than suicide would be for a happy child. Therefore the afflicted are not listened to. . . .

That is why there is no hope for the vagrant as he stands before the magistrate. Even if, through his stammerings, he should utter a cry to pierce the soul, neither the magistrate nor the public will hear it. His cry is mute. And the afflicted are nearly always equally deaf to one another;

and each of them, constrained by the general indifference, strives by means of self-delusion or forgetfulness to become deaf to his own self.

Only by the supernatural working of grace can a soul pass through its own annihilation to the place where alone it can get the sort of attention which can attend to truth and to affliction. It is the same attention which listens to both of them. The name of this intense, pure, disinterested, gratuitous, generous attention is love.

Simone Weil (6, 30–31)

The silence of the Christian is listening silence, humble stillness, that may be interrupted at any time for the sake of humility.

Dietrich Bonhoeffer (4, 80)

But has not the moment passed when God speaks in the desert, and must we not now understand that "He who is" is not to be heard in this place or that, for the heights where He dwells are not inaccessible mountains but a more profound sphere of things? The secret of the world lies wherever we can discern the transparency of the universe.

Pierre Teilhard de Chardin (2, 66)

The more faithfully you listen to the voice within you, the better you will hear what is sounding outside. And only he who listens can speak. Is this the starting point of the road towards the union of your two dreams— to be allowed in clarity of mind to mirror life and in purity of heart to mold it?

Dag Hammarskjöld (13)

Caught up as most of us are in the complexities of daily living, we forget that we are surrounded by the creative power of Love. Every once in a while we need to step aside from the troubles and pleasures of our lives, and take a fresh look, a time to feel, and listen to our Source.

Madeleine L'Engle (1, 15)

God often speaks to us at night, when we have let down our defenses and are quiet enough to hear his voice. When we try to take control of our lives, and perhaps the lives of some of the people around us, our eyes and ears are closed to God's visions.

Madeleine L'Engle (1, 122)

In this life of waiting and of trusting, of attending entirely to Jesus' will for us and to his love for us living in simplicity with the brothers and the sisters, in the breaking of bread and in mutual love, we learn gradually to experience a new dimension of our Christian life.

Thomas Merton (4, 380–81)

Attentiveness is not tenseness or strained effort but presence and relaxation, quietness and receptivity, presence with, love. Attentiveness can be learned. We can become sensitized to attentiveness.

A Carthusian (97)

Attentiveness is the natural prayer of the mind that seeks truth. It is waiting, pure receptivity. It unconditionally welcomes the truth, whatever it may be. It does not interpose preconceptions, concerns or fears. The ineluctable conditions for attentiveness are an awakened mind that watches for the light, a thirst for truth, integrity and a brave heart, silence and solitude.

A Carthusian (97)

When you walk, walk. When you pray, pray. When you look, look. When you eat, eat.

The secret of life is quite simply to live it. The present moment holds inexhaustible richness. Attentiveness is the key to living profoundly. This depth is not confined to an esoteric sphere, but is at the heart of the daily round—precisely in its ordinariness.

There are several kinds of attentiveness depending on whether the attention is directed towards things, towards interior ideas and images, towards others, towards itself, towards God.

A Carthusian (99)

Attentiveness to self and attentiveness to God are like two interdependent and complementary movements, the breathing of our deepest being: Lord Jesus (attentiveness to God)—have mercy on me, a sinner (attentiveness to self).

A Carthusian (107)

Attentiveness to God is rather to be receptive to this divine light, which shines in the face of Christ and shines by grace in our hearts, than an activity of the intellect. It is above all poverty, faith, receptive emptiness, nakedness and freedom. It is eyes that are open in the dark, the desire of love.

A Carthusian (107)

Listening to God has a dreamlike quality. Oh, you are awake. But you are at work. It is an interiorized situation in which he comes to you and clears a little bit of your heart. He makes it comfortable there for himself and there he talks to you as a friend to a friend. . . . It is as if God came to prepare you again and again to listen to men.

Catherine de Hueck Doherty (161)

So, unharness. Relax. For half a minute every two hours, stop! Put down what you have in your hand. Hold yourself straight. Breathe deeply. Draw your senses inward. Suspend yourself before the inner dark, the inner void. And even if nothing happens, you will have broken the chain of haste. . . .

It is unlikely that in so short a time you will plunge deeply into the mystery of self, but it is not impossible with the grace of God. However, even if nothing else happens during the moment of suspension, we shall at least have broken the chain of events that held us prisoner. We shall have broken it in six and taken the first step toward deliverance.

Lanza del Vasto (1, 27–28)

It is not enough to pay attention to what you are doing. You must pay attention to yourself doing what you are doing.

Lanza del Vasto (1, 34–35)

To consider oneself worthy of consideration and to behave with self-assurance and self-importance is simply to forget God.

Lanza del Vasto (1, 87)

A friend of mine who is a priest was meditating one day upon these same Emmaus disciples. He found it difficult to believe that after three years of living with Jesus they failed to recognize him when he joined them and began talking to them.

When there is a real friendship with someone, we are able to recognize them by the way they walk, their voice or even a cough.

My friend was meditating on this when there came a knock at the door. It was a poor person who wanted to tell his troubles to a priest.

The priest, immersed in his meditation upon the disciples of Emmaus, asked to be excused for not being able to listen to the poor man. He was, he said, really very busy. He even gave the man more money than he would have done normally, and went back to his meditation.

Soon afterwards it dawned on him that he had done exactly what the disciples at Emmaus had done: "Christ knocked at my door. I saw him, I heard him, I talked to him and I failed to recognize him."

Dom Helder Camara (3, 42–44)

While Jesus predicts that people will die of fear "as they await what menaces the world" (Luke 21:26), he says to his followers: "Stay awake, praying at all times for the strength to survive all that is going to happen, and to stand with confidence before the Son of Man" (Luke 21:36). After I have looked for a long time at Rublev's Trinity, these words have come to speak to me with new power. "Praying at all times" has come to mean "dwelling in the house of God all the days of our lives." "Surviving all that is going to happen" now tells me that I no longer need to be a victim of the fear, hatred, and violence that rule the world. "Standing with confidence before the Son of Man" no longer just refers to the end of all times but opens for me the possibility of living confidently, that is, with trust (the literal meaning of con-fide) in the midst of hostility and violence.

Henri Nouwen (9, 9)

To begin again with God means seeing that we cannot go on as we are. To build again with God means that we cannot go running or creeping on in the old groove, in the old, bad, accustomed routine. It means looking to see if God's light and power are not visible, and they are often closer than we think. It means waiting. . . not in the void, but for God's redemption, for the bars of our prison to burst open suddenly. Jesus has summoned God's kingdom into real life as the surest and most real of all things.

Karl Barth (7, 99–100)

The first service that one owes to others in the fellowship consists in listening to them. Just as love to God begins with listening to His Word, so the beginning of love for the brethren is learning to listen to them. It is God's love for us that He not only gives us His Word but also lends us His ear.

Dietrich Bonhoeffer (4, 97)

Parallel Scripture Passages

Matthew 4:1–17
John 10:27–30
Deuteronomy 4:29–31
Revelation 22:17
Psalm 85:8–9
Luke 8:4–15

Revelation 3:13–22
Isaiah 6:1–9
Luke 11:27–28
Luke 2:19
Isaiah 50:4–5
Jeremiah 7:1–11

Psalm 105:1–5
Deuteronomy 6:4–13
Jeremiah 7:22–28
Hebrews 3:7–13
Luke 9:28–36
Matthew 7:21–27

Community, Communion, and Church

There is no better symbol of communal life than the banquet.

Martin Buber (3, 77)

The only answer in this life, to the loneliness we are all bound to feel, is community. The living together, working together, sharing together, loving God and loving our brother, and living close to him in community so we can show our love for Him.

Dorothy Day (243)

A real community need not consist of people who are perpetually together; but it must consist of people who, precisely because they are comrades, have mutual access to one another and are ready for one another.

Martin Buber (3, 145)

Community ... cannot occur once and for all time: always it must be the moment's answer to the moment's question, and nothing more.

Martin Buber (3, 134)

Community is the inner disposition or constitution of a life in common, which knows and embraces in itself hard "calculation", adverse "chance", the sudden access of "anxiety". It is community of tribulation and only because of that community of spirit; community of toil and only because of that community of salvation. Even those communities which call the spirit their master and salvation their Promised Land, the "religious" communities, are community only if they serve their lord and master in the midst of simple, unexalted, unselected reality, a reality not so much chosen by them as sent to them just as it is; they are community only if they prepare the way to the Promised Land through the thickets of this pathless hour. . . . A community of faith truly exists only when it is a community of work.

Martin Buber (3, 134–35)

The architects must be set the task of also building for human contact, building surroundings that invite meeting and centers that shape meeting.

Martin Buber (1, 95)

The Apostolic Community: It is difficult to believe all alone, it is hardly possible to live a faith in Love all alone. The first community of Christians in Jerusalem relied on the golden rule for monks of every age. In this first springtime, the grace of Christ flowered with an exquisite flower of unity and fraternity. In the inexhaustible youth of the Spirit it is always springtime. It can be so with us, if only we will open our hearts. "They devoted themselves to the apostles' teaching and fellowship, to the breaking of bread and the prayers. . . . All who believed were together and had all things in common; they would sell their possessions and goods and distribute the proceeds to all, as any had need. Day by day, as they spent much time together in the temple, they broke bread at home and ate their food with glad and generous hearts, praising God and having the goodwill of all the people. And day by day the Lord added to their number those who were being saved" (Acts 2:42–47).

A Carthusian, 21st Conference 1978[1]

The Church exists by *happening.* The Church exists as the *event* of this *gathering together.*

Karl Barth (6, 62)

The Christian community . . . the Church . . . exists only as a definite history takes place, . . . only as it is gathered and lets itself be gathered and gathers itself by the living Jesus Christ through the Holy Spirit. . . . Its act is its being, its status its dynamic, its essence its existence. The Church *is* when it takes place that God lets certain men live as His servants, His friends, His children, the witnesses of the reconciliation of the world with Himself as it has taken place in Jesus Christ. . . . The Church *is* when it happens. . . . The Church *is* when these men subject themselves to the law of the Gospel, "the law of the Spirit of life" (Rom. 8:2).

Karl Barth (3, 650–51)

The Church *is* when it takes place, and it takes place in the form of a sequence and nexus of definite human activities.

Karl Barth (3, 652)

The real essence of community is to be found in the fact . . . that it has a centre. The real beginning of a community is when its members have a common relation to the centre overriding all other relations. . . . The centre cannot be discerned unless it is discerned as being transpicuous to the light of something divine. All this is true; but the more earthly, the more creaturely, the more attached the centre is, the truer and more transpicuous it will be.

Martin Buber (3, 135)

Silent listening was only the beginning of community. It instituted community; and, as always, here too there had to be continual return to the original institution, so that by this summoning to concentration new strength could again and again be drawn from the depths of the beginning. But the inner life of community does not begin and end with this initial silent listening. This life is born only in an act which is essentially a renewal. Not in a mere repetition of a beginning once created, but in the re-creating of what has grown effete. The re-creating of bodily life, the transformation of matter grown old, occurs in the course of a meal. Even for the individual, eating and drinking ·constitute rebirth for the body. For the community, the meal taken in common is the action through which it is reborn to conscious life.

The silent *community of hearing* and heeding establishes even the smallest community, that of the household. The household is based on the circumstance that the word of the father of the family is heard and heeded. Still, the *common life* of the household does not become manifest in the common heeding but in the meal at which all the members of the house gather round the table. Here each is the equal of every other; each lives for himself and yet is joined with all the others. It is not table talk that establishes this community, for in many rural districts it is not customary to speak during the meal, it is even contrary to custom. Talking at table does not, at any rate, establish community; at most it expresses it. One can talk in the street and in the square wherever people meet haphazardly. The common meal with its silent community represents actual community alive in the midst of life.

Franz Rosenzweig (316–17)

Wherever the early Christians entered a town the power structure got disturbed and immediately sought to convict them for being "disturbers of the peace" and "outside agitators." But they went on with the conviction that they were a "colony of heaven" and had to obey God rather than man. They were small in number but big in commitment. . . .

. . . If the Church of today does not recapture the sacrificial spirit of the early Church, it will lose its authentic ring, forfeit the loyalty of millions, and be dismissed as an irrelevant social club with no meaning for the twentieth century. I am meeting young people every day whose disappointment with the Church has risen to outright disgust.

Martin Luther King Jr. (2, 12)

By her [the church's] own silence she has rendered herself guilty of the decline in responsible action, in bravery in the defence of a cause, and in willingness to suffer for what is known to be right. She bears the guilt of the defection of the governing authority from Christ.

Dietrich Bonhoeffer (2, 51)

With a young humanity all across the globe, you are eagerly waiting for the frontiers that separate peoples to be brought down. Going to visit one another: what a festival! Unless we know each other, how can we let confidence and sharing be born; how can we heal divisions, be reconciled; how can we join the Risen Christ in his pilgrimage through humanity as the Crucified Lord? Until the end of time he remains beside all who are going through times of trial.

Brother Roger, "Letter from Warsaw,"[2] *Letter from Taizé,* February 1982

A new organizational paradigm [for the church] is useless and its implementation reverts to former ills unless its foundations rest on the humility of Christ, of *kenosis*, of eucharistic ungraspingness, unless the people of God are educated to cherish self-forgetful, awestruck wonder before the humble God from the beginning of their coming to the community.

Maggie Ross (3, 167)

The eucharistic community includes all of creation. The Body of Christ is the fundamental resonance of humility, of self-giving, that is, sacrificial *kenosis* that leads to creation and re-creation, no matter in what sphere. It is the cohesion of creation.

Maggie Ross (3, 167)

Each bit of creation is sustained by the life of God, is sacrament, and is engaged with the whole of creation. Each moment of life can be and, if we are committed to the humility of Christ, *must* be Eucharist.

Maggie Ross (3, 166)

Human being is being with other humans. Apart from this relationship we become inhuman. We are human by being together, by seeing, hearing, speaking with, and standing by, one another as men [and women], insofar, that is, as we do this gladly and thus do it freely.

Karl Barth (6, 6)

[Easter Sunday 1970 announcement of the worldwide Council of Youth]

The risen Christ comes to quicken, to bring alive, a festival in the innermost heart of man.

He is preparing for us a springtime of the Church—a Church devoid of the means of power, ready to share with all men, a place of visible communion for the whole of humanity.

He is going to give us enough imagination and courage to open up a way of reconciliation, of unity.

He is going to prepare us to give our lives so that man be no longer victim of man.

Brother Roger, Letter From Taizé, spring 1970

True communion, true community is not a matter of push-me-pull-you togetherness and destructive dependence relationships but rather what the poet Rilke has described as the meeting of solitudes who know the extravagance of walking unembraced. This acknowledging of otherness is the prerequisite of true union and knowledge of what is meant by the Body of Christ.

Maggie Ross (2, 56)

The Eucharist must invade my life. My life must become, as a result of the sacrament, an unlimited and endless contact with you—that life which seemed, a few moments ago, like a baptism with you in the waters of the world, now reveals itself to me as communion with you through the world. It is the sacrament of life. The sacrament of my life—*of my life received, of my life lived, of my life surrendered. . . .*

Pierre Teilhard de Chardin (1, 126–27)

Christ gave us the sacraments in order that we might better keep the two great commandments. . . . The center of this is the Eucharist.

Flannery O'Connor (1, 346)

It is vitally important, therefore, that the wealthier states, in providing varied forms of assistance to the poorer, should respect the moral values and ethnic characteristics peculiar to each, and also that they should avoid any intention of political domination. If this is done, *a precious contribution will be made towards the formation of a world community, a community in which each member, whilst conscious of its own individual rights and duties, will work in a relationship of equality towards the attainment of the universal common good.*

Pope John XXIII (2, 29)

The community of faith offers the protective boundaries within which we can listen to our deepest longings, not to indulge in morbid introspection, but to find our God to whom they point. In the community of faith we can listen to our feelings of loneliness, to our desires for an embrace or a kiss, to our sexual urges, to our cravings for sympathy, compassion or just a good word; also to our search for insight and to our hope for companionship and friendship. In the community of faith we can listen to all these longings and find the courage, not to avoid them or cover them up, but to confront them in order to discern God's presence in their midst. There we can affirm each other in our waiting and also in the realization that in the center of our waiting the first intimacy with God is found.

Henri Nouwen (8, 109)

This eternal community of love is the center and source of Jesus' spiritual life, a life of uninterrupted attentiveness to the Father in the Spirit of love. It is from this life that Jesus' ministry grows. His eating and fasting, his praying and acting, his traveling and resting, his preaching and teaching, his exorcising and healing, were all done in this Spirit of love. We will never understand the full meaning of Jesus' richly varied ministry unless we see how the many things are rooted in the one thing: listening to the Father in the intimacy of perfect love. When we see this, we will also realize that the goal of Jesus' ministry is nothing less than to bring us into this most intimate community.

Henri Nouwen (6, 49–50)

Will your home, or your room, be the "house of Zacchaeus" [Luke 19:1–10]: a house of forgiveness, a parable of reconciliation? . . .

. . . At a time when so many young people around you find it hard to overcome insinuating doubt and are deserting the churches, the inconsistency of the divisions between Christians adds an additional burden. . . . You want to do all you can so that the conflicts between Christians do not imprison those young people who are persevering in that communion of communions which is the Body of Christ, his Church, a contemplative people.

Brother Roger, "Letter from Warsaw," *Letter from Taizé*, February, 1982

Through fellowship and communion with the incarnate Lord, we recover our true humanity, and at the same time we are delivered from that individualism which is the consequence of sin, and retrieve our solidarity with the whole human race. By being partakers of Christ incarnate, we are partakers in the whole humanity which he bore.

Dietrich Bonhoeffer (1, 272)

"The Body of Christ," George says, placing the wafer on my tongue. The words both describe this scrap of bread and affirm my identity: a double mystery. I eat the Body of Christ. I am—we are all—the Body of Christ. Nourished by God, we must bear God into the world and give God away with ourselves.

Nancy Mairs (139)

The Eucharist is the sacrament of prayer, the source and summit of the Christian life. His presence before us hastens His cumulative presence in us. His presence imparts the Spirit to us, and lights up the shadows of our heart in deep communion.

The Holy Hour before the Eucharist should lead us to a "holy hour" with the poor, with those who will never be a human success and whose only consolation is Jesus. Our Eucharist is incomplete if it does not make us love and serve the poor. In receiving the communion of the poor, we discover our own poverty.

Mother Teresa of Calcutta (1, 19)

Parallel Scripture Passages

1 Corinthians 12:24b–26	Acts 2:44–47
Isaiah 65:17–25	1 Corinthians 10:16–17
Ephesians 4:1–6	Colossians 1:1–17
1 Corinthians 12:1–27	1 Corinthians 10:16
Matthew 26:17–29	2 Corinthians 13:13
Matthew 3:1–17	1 Corinthians 11:23–33

Contemplation and Action

In our era, the road to holiness necessarily passes through the world of action.

Dag Hammarskjöld (122)

Breathing, meditation, contemplation—these are all attempts of the soul to "make an exit out of the world, out of the flesh, out of all mental objects, then finally out of myself, that is, out of one's own will," attempts to make the dominant "I" smaller, to become "I-less," so that we can come to ourselves.

Dorothee Soelle (2, 79)

The true inner life makes the active life burn forth and consume everything. It makes us find Jesus in the dark holes of the slums, in the most pitiful miseries of the poor, in the God-man naked on the cross, mournful, despised by all, the man of suffering, crushed like a worm by the scourging and the crucifixion.

Mother Teresa of Calcutta (1, 110)

In contemplation, the right relationship with God is love, in action it is slavery. This distinction must be kept. We must act as becomes a slave while contemplating with love.

Simone Weil (2, 44)

The monk is not defined by his task, his usefulness. In a certain sense he is supposed to be "useless" because his mission is not to *do* this or that job but to *be* a man of God. He does not live in order to exercise a specific function: his business is life itself. . . . The monk seeks to be free from what William Faulkner called "the same frantic steeplechase toward nothing" which is the essence of "worldliness" everywhere.

Thomas Merton (4, 27)

Contemplation . . . frees us from self-seeking. . . . It is something vital for any person wishing to undertake daring political actions. It enables him to refrain from seeking ways of imposing his own ideas, and not to desire unconsciously his own success, but only to serve.

Brother Roger (3, 71)

The whole purpose of monastic obedience . . . is the sanctification of the monk and in fact his liberation from temporal agitations and concerns in order that he may learn to listen to God in his heart and to obey God.

Thomas Merton (4, 137–38)

The Listening Heart: God penetrates our heart "by every path and opportunity." This requires from us a habitually tranquil and listening heart. This is the fundamental attitude of the contemplative: an attitude of receptivity, open at every level to listening; not only or even primarily of the intellect but of the heart. It isn't so much a matter of seeking God by our activity, of placing a hand on God, as allowing God to give himself to us. And God is present in everything and through everything gives himself: in his Word, in the sacraments of the faith, in prayer, in our brothers, in sunlight, in the snow's purity, in joy and sorrow, in silence, in the chant, in the harmony of forms, in the mystery of suffering. Everything is Word of God, Christ has assumed everything, made everything sacrament, symbol, sign. Let us learn to welcome him in everything, let us continually cultivate and deepen our capacity to receive him at every level. Let us at all times have awakened and enlarging hearts. Nothing is inconsequential, nothing is indifferent, everything is vast—if we perceive the gift of God!

A Carthusian, 25th Conference, 1979[1]

Contemplation . . . is a deep resonance in the inmost center of our spirit in which our very life loses its separate voice and re-sounds with the majesty and the mercy of the Hidden and Living One. He answers Himself in us and this answer is divine life, divine creativity, making all things new. We ourselves become His echo and His answer.

Thomas Merton (6, 3)

Christian action must, if it wants to deserve this name and be distinguished from secular action, come from much more than simply human compassion; it must come from the knowledge of and gratitude for God's compassion on the cross, and it must be prepared to go even farther: to the point of suffering, of participating in the cross. Christian action is a mediating link between the offering of oneself in prayer and the giving of oneself to be disposed of entirely according to God's will.

Hans Urs von Balthasar (327)

The hermitage . . . provides the monk with something that a mature person needs: the chance to explore, to risk, to abandon himself sagaciously to untried possibilities. This is one of the most important aspects of the wilderness theme in the Bible and in the history of the People of God.

Thomas Merton (4, 258)

A mystic is a child at play—the mystic within us is the child within us.

Matthew Fox (2, 60)

In the contemplative life every conflict, inner or outer, small or large, can be seen as the tip of an iceberg, the expressive part of something deeper and larger. It is worthwhile, even necessary to explore that which is underneath the surface of our daily actions, thoughts, and feelings.

Henri Nouwen (1, 64)

Each time you let the love of God penetrate deeper into your heart, you lose a bit of your anxiety, and every time you shed a bit of your anxiety, you learn to know yourself better and long all the more to be known by your loving God.

Henri Nouwen (3, 68–69)

Saintliness means living without division between word and action. If I would truly live in my own life the word I am speaking, my spoken words would become actions, and miracles would happen whenever I opened my mouth. The Gospel of today thus confronts me not so much with a question about pastoral tactics or strategy, but with an invitation to deep personal conversion.

Henri Nouwen (2, 125)

Parallel Scripture Passages

John 14:6–15
Matthew 25:31–46
John 14:23
1 Corinthians 13:1–13
John 15:1–11

GLEANINGS

Faith and Hope

HOPE IS A DIMENSION OF THE SPIRIT. It is not outside us, but within us. When you lose it, you must seek it again WITHIN YOURSELF and in people around you—not in objects or even in events.

Václav Havel (1, 53)

When faith is completely replaced by creed, worship by discipline, love by habit; when the crisis of today is ignored because of the splendor of the past; when faith becomes an heirloom rather than a living fountain; when religion speaks only in the name of authority rather than with the voice of compassion—its message becomes meaningless.

Abraham Heschel (3)

The odd thing was that before God closed in on me, I was in fact offered what now appears a moment of wholly free choice. In a sense. I was going up Headington Hill on the top of a bus. Without words and (I think) almost without images, a fact about myself was somehow presented to me. I became aware that I was holding something at bay, or shutting something out. Or, if you like, that I was wearing some stiff clothing, like corsets, or even a suit of armor, as if I were a lobster. I felt myself being, there and then, given a free choice.

C. S. Lewis (4, 224)

I need Christ, not something that resembles Him. . . . A really good photograph might become in the end a snare, a horror, and an obstacle.

C. S. Lewis (1, 76)

In Louisville, at the corner of Fourth and Walnut, in the center of the shopping district, I was suddenly overwhelmed with the realization that I loved all those people, that they were mine and I theirs, that we could not be alien to one another even though we were total strangers. It was like waking from a dream of separateness, of spurious self-isolation in a special world, the world of renunciation and supposed holiness. The whole illusion of a separate holy existence is a dream. . . .

This sense of liberation from an illusory difference was such a relief and such a joy to me that I almost laughed out loud.

It is a glorious destiny to be a member of the human race, though it is a race dedicated to many absurdities and one which makes many terrible mistakes: yet, with all that, God Himself gloried in becoming a member of the human race. A member of the human race! To think that such a commonplace realization should suddenly seem like news that one holds the winning ticket in a cosmic sweepstake. . . .

There is no way of telling people that they are all walking around shining like the sun.

There are no strangers!

If only we could see each other [as we really are] . . . all the time. There would be no more war, no more hatred, no more cruelty, no more greed. . . . I suppose the big problem would be that we would fall down and worship each other. . . .

The gate of heaven is everywhere.

Thomas Merton (3, 140–42)

Faith consists in the acceptance of doubts, the working through them, rather than the repression of them.

Madeleine L'Engle (1, 51)

Trust again and again and again, as God trusts us. If man gives his trust to another, and people give their trust to people, then the very act of trusting can make another person a bit more trustworthy than they were before. As the trust continues—joyous, smiling, simple, ordinary trust— the one to whom it is given begins to straighten up and look at himself and find in himself something he never thought of finding before—that he is trustworthy in spite of his failings! He realizes this because someone trusts him!

Catherine de Hueck Doherty (189)

God does not accept praise, gifts and honours from those who have no eye or heart for the human family, his sons and daughters of all races, all colours, all languages and creeds. . . . No one was created to be a slave or a beggar.

Dom Helder Camara (3, 22)

Our task is to bring God back into the world, into our lives. To worship is to expand the presence of God in the world. To have faith in God is to reveal what is concealed.

Abraham Heschel (156–57)

To be a Christian is to accept and to live—in solidarity, in faith, hope and charity—the meaning that the Word of the Lord and our encounter with him give to the historical becoming of mankind on the way toward total communion. To regard the unique and absolute relationship with God as the horizon of every human action is to place oneself, from the outset, in a wider and more profound context.

Gustavo Gutiérrez (1, 49–50)

Where there is the great hope, necessarily there are small hopes for the immediate future. These hopes have their basis and strength only in the great hope. . . . But within these limits they are genuine hopes. And it is certainly in these many little hopes that the Christian lives from day to day if he really lives in the great hope. . . . [The Christian] is daily willing and ready for the small and provisional and imperfect service of God which the immediate future will demand of him because a great and final and perfect being in the service of God is the future of the world and all men, and therefore his future also.

Karl Barth (3, 121–22)

This may be a better age for the Faith, but this is certainly not an age of Faith.

Flannery O'Connor (1, 152)

What people don't realize is how much religion costs. They think faith is a big electric blanket, when of course it is the cross. It is much harder to believe than not to believe. If you feel you can't believe, you must at least do this: keep an open mind. Keep it open toward faith, keep wanting it, keep asking for it, and leave the rest to God.

Flannery O'Connor (1, 354)

Or is it [the redemption of the cross] this way: is my surrender to the crushing narrowness of earthly existence the beginning of my liberation from it, precisely because this surrender is my "Amen" to Your human life, my way of saying "Yes" to Your human coming, which happens in a manner so contrary to my expectations?

Karl Rahner (1, 85)

Even in the life of a Christian, faith rises and falls like the tides of an invisible sea. It's there, even when he can't see it or feel it, if he wants it to be there. You realize, I think, that it is more valuable, more mysterious, altogether more immense than anything you can learn or decide upon in college. Learn what you can, but cultivate Christian scepticism. It will keep you free—not free to do anything you please, but free to be formed by something larger than your own intellect or the intellects of those around you.

Flannery O'Connor (1, 477–78)

Faith is the touching of a mystery, it is to perceive another dimension to absolutely everything in the world. In faith, the mysterious meaning of life comes alive. Beneath the simple, explicable, one-dimensional surface of things their genuine content begins to shine. Nature herself begins to speak out and to witness to what is above her, within her, but *separate from her*. To speak in the simplest possible terms: faith sees, knows, senses . . . the presence of God in the world.

Alexander Schmemann (1, 59–60)

The Christian life is but a constant re-beginning, a return to grace every day, sometimes even every hour, through Him who, after each failure, pardons so that all things should be made new.

Brother Roger (2, 29)

A winter ago I had an after-school seminar for high-school students and in one of the early sessions Una, a brilliant fifteen-year-old, a born writer who came to Harlem from Panama five years ago, and only then discovered the conflict between races, asked me out of the blue: "Mrs. Franklin, do you really and truly believe in God with no doubts at all?"

"Oh, Una, I really and truly believe in God with all kinds of doubts."

But I base my life on this belief.

Madeleine L'Engle (2, 63)

Every moment and every event of every man's life on earth plants something in his soul. For just as the wind carries thousands of winged seeds, so each moment brings with it germs of spiritual vitality that come to rest imperceptibly in the minds and wills of men. Most of these unnumbered seeds perish and are lost, because men are not prepared to receive them: for such seeds as these cannot spring up anywhere except in the good soil of freedom, spontaneity and love.

Thomas Merton (6, 14)

The meaning of faith in the New Testament . . . is not just acquiescence in the story of Christ with its moral and spiritual implications. It is not merely the decision to put into practice, to some extent at least, the teachings of Christ. . . .

But the real meaning of faith is *the rejection of everything that is not Christ in order that all life, all truth, all hope, all reality may be sought and found "in Christ."*

Thomas Merton (5, 78)

The final step on the way to holiness in Christ is then to completely abandon ourselves with confident joy to the apparent madness of the cross . . . (I Cor. 1:18). This madness, the folly of abandoning all concern for ourselves both in the material and in the spiritual order, that we may entrust ourselves to Christ, means a kind of death to our temporal selves. It is a twisting, a letting go, an act of total abandonment. But it is also a final break-through into joy. The ability to make this act, to let go, to plunge into our own emptiness and there find the freedom of Christ in all fullness—this is inaccessible to all our merely human efforts and plans. We cannot do it by relaxing or by striving, by thinking or not thinking, by acting or not acting. The only answer is perfect faith, exultant hope, transformed by a completely spiritual love of Christ. This is a pure gift of his: but we can dispose ourselves to receive it by fortitude, humility, patience, and, above all, by simple fidelity to his will in every circumstance of our ordinary life.

Thomas Merton (5, 119)

One of the favorite images I like to use for describing the Christian life is of a person standing with arms outstretched. One hand, in faith and prayer, touches God; the other hand is extended in service to the neighbor. Thus is a person cruciform, touching God and touching neighbor. It seemed that the words which came to me in the poustinia revolved around these two themes.

Catherine de Hueck Doherty (148)

Faith walks simply, childlike, between the darkness of human life and the hope of what is to come. "For eye has not seen, nor ear heard what God reserves for those who love him." Faith is fundamentally a kind of folly, I guess, the folly that belongs to God himself.

Catherine de Hueck Doherty (150)

To believe in God means to take sides with life and to end our alliance with death. It means to stop killing and wanting to kill, and to do battle with apathy which is so akin to killing. . . .

Taking sides with life is not an easy or simple thing. It involves a never-ending process of change whereby we constantly renounce the self that is dead and enamored of death and instead become free to love life.

Dorothee Soelle (2, 10)

It is up to you, then, to anticipate a reconciliation without delay. Anticipating is an expression of hope. It means living out already, here and now, what one is hoping for. Until the twilight of your years, nothing is better able to keep your heart attentive and forever young.

Brother Roger, "Letter from Warsaw," *Letter from Taizé*, February 1982

Parallel Scripture Passages

Psalm 27:1–14	Lamentations 3:22–26
Psalm 43:3–5	Hebrews 11:1–3
Psalm 62:5–8	Isaiah 25:4–9
Psalm 85:10–13	Isaiah 35:1–10

GLEANINGS

Holiness and Spirituality

The spiritual life is like a dance with a partner who has a fertile imagination and who leads. We must be alert, responsive to the slightest indication of his intention, supple, ready to adapt to the movements with which he woos us.

A Carthusian (78)

"Pour into our hearts the attitude of your love." Pour it in: become yourself one flowing for us, for our flowing does not carry us to you. Be rain in our dryness; be a river through our landscape so that it might have in you its center as well as the cause of its growing and bearing fruit. And if your water brings both blossoms and fruit in us, then we do not want to consider them as our own drives and results, because they come from you; and we want to consign them in advance to the invisible goods with you, over which you can dispose as you will.

Hans Urs von Balthasar (428)

God is so close to us, around us, in us. The wind that caresses our face, the bird that sings, the mountain touching the heavens, an exquisite flower among the rocks, the immense sky, silence that trembles in its fullness, a smile, a look of love—all speak of the creator, *infundens esse,* leaving everywhere the marks of his passage. And ourselves: he is the source of our being and is more intimate with us than we are with our own souls.

A Carthusian (14)

There is no true human share of holiness without the hallowing of the everyday.

Martin Buber (4, 270)

Spirituality is . . . like living water that springs up in the very depth of the experience of faith.

Gustavo Gutiérrez (2, 37)

A spirituality is a walking in freedom according to the Spirit of love and life.

Gustavo Gutiérrez (2, 35)

This is what we mean by the term *spiritual:* It is the reference to the transcendent in our own existence, the direction of the Here toward the Beyond. It is the ecstatic force that stirs all our goals, redeeming values from the narrowness of being ends in themselves, turning arrivals into new pilgrimages, new farings forth. It is an all-pervading trend that both contains and transcends all values, a never-ending process, the upward movement of being. The spiritual is not something we own, but something we may share in. We do not possess it; we may be possessed by it. When we perceive it, it is as if our mind were gliding for a while with an eternal current, in which our ideas become knowledge swept beyond itself.

Abraham Heschel (416)

When superimposed as a yoke, as a dogma, as a fear, religion tends to violate rather than to nurture the spirit of man. Religion must be an altar upon which the fire of the soul may be kindled in holiness.

Abraham Heschel (317)

Holiness is the sanctification of ordinary life.

Maggie Ross (1, 139)

Holiness is the descent of divinity into the midst of our concrete world—
"For the Lord thy God walketh in the midst of thy camp . . . therefore

shall thy camp be holy" (Deut. 23:15). . . . The dream of creation finds its resolution in the actualization of the principle of holiness. Creation means the realization of the ideal of holiness.

Joseph Soloveitchik (2, 108)

To have found God is not an end but in itself a beginning.

Franz Rosenzweig (xviii–xix)

For everyone there should be enough room, enough freedom to plan the use of one's time, the opportunity to reach ever higher levels of attention, some solitude, some silence. At the same time everyone needs warmth, lest it be driven by distress to submerge itself in the collective. . . . What man needs is silence and warmth; what he is given is an icy pandemonium.

Simone Weil (6, 20–21)

The essential aims of life are present naturally in every person. In everyone there is some longing for humanity's rightful dignity, for moral integrity, for free expression of being and a sense of transcendence over the world of existence. Yet, at the same time, each person is capable, to a greater or lesser degree, of coming to terms with living within the lie. Each person somehow succumbs to a profane trivialization of his or her inherent humanity, and to utilitarianism.

Václav Havel (2, 54)

There can be no transitory human existence without the horizon of permanence against which it develops and to which—whether it knows this or not—it constantly relates.

Václav Havel (1, 147)

We are a little like a blind man touching the woman he loves, whom he has never seen and never will. The question of the meaning of life, then, is not a full stop at the end of life, but the beginning of a deeper experience of life. It is like a light whose source we cannot see, but in whose illumination we nevertheless live—whether we delight in its incomprehensible abundance or suffer from its incomprehensible dearth.

Václav Havel (1, 225)

At the bottom of the heart of every human being, from earliest infancy until the tomb, there is something that goes on indomitably expecting, in the teeth of all experience of crimes committed, suffered, and witnessed, that good and not evil will be done to him. It is this above all that is sacred in every human being.

Simone Weil (6, 14)

Whence comes this strange and clearly impractical and "unrealistic" essence of the moral law, that which is called "good"? I think the answer is clear: that curious feeling of "responsibility for the world" can probably only be felt by someone who is really (consciously or unconsciously) in touch, within himself, with "the absolute horizon of Being," who communicates or struggles with it in some way, who draws from it meaning, hope and faith, who has genuinely (through inner experience) grasped it. . . . In other words: by perceiving ourselves as part of the river, we accept our responsibility for the river as a whole (which is folly in the eyes of all proprietors of dams and particular horizons).

Václav Havel (1, 301)

Of this I am certain: of our calling to holiness, our vocation to persist, in season and out in the work of healing others, even as we seek healing for ourselves. . . .

So we take heart. We commend the woman who quite simply, with all her heart, on behalf of someone she loved, refused to give up [the Syrophoenician woman, Mark 7:24–30]. We might think of her act as a "forgiving persistence" toward Christ. We might also wish to ponder a kind of "persistent forgiveness" toward the church.

The woman refuses and persists. And so prevails.

And so must we. And so shall we.

We must forgive, deepen our love, persist in our conviction that even the church can be redeemed from sin.

In so fulfilling our vocation, we ourselves are healed.

Daniel Berrigan (4, 230–31)

The work of the Holy Spirit is that our blind eyes are opened and that thankfully and in thankful self-surrender we recognize and acknowledge that it is so: Amen.

Karl Barth (1, 239)

The story is told that the once famous Professor Tholuck of Halle used to visit the rooms of his students and press them with the question, "Brother, how are things in your heart?" How do things stand with you yourself?—not with your ears, not with your head, not with your forensic ability, not with your industriousness. . . . In biblical terms the question is precisely, "How are things with your *heart*?" It is the question very properly addressed to every young and old theologian!

Karl Barth (4, 83)

It is not our business to withdraw from the world before our time; rather let us learn to orientate our being in the flux of things; then, instead of the force of gravity which drags us down to the abyss of self-indulgence and selfishness, we shall feel a salutary "component" emerge from created things which, by a process we have already described, will enlarge our horizons, will snatch us away from our pettinesses and impel us imperiously towards a widening of our vision, towards the renunciation of cherished pleasure, towards the desire for ever more spiritual beauty.

Pierre Teilhard de Chardin (1, 108–9)

Every believer in this world of ours must be a spark of light, a center of love, a vivifying leaven amidst his fellowmen: and he will be this all the more perfectly the more closely he lives in communion with God and in the intimacy of his own soul.

In fact, there can be no peace between men unless there is peace within each one of them, unless, that is, each one builds up within himself the order wished by God.

Pope John XXIII (2, 40)

Whatever you do anyway, remember that these things are mysteries and that if they were such that we could understand them, they wouldn't be worth understanding. A God you understood would be less than yourself.

Flannery O'Connor (1, 354)

Beside our need for a meaning, also a need for human intimacy without conventional trappings—for the experience of a circle where power expresses itself in meaningful and beautiful forms. The holiness of human life, before which we bow down in worship.

Dag Hammarskjöld (99)

In the point of rest at the center of our being, we encounter a world where all things are at rest in the same way. Then a tree becomes a mystery, a cloud a revelation, each man a cosmos of whose riches we can only catch glimpses. The life of simplicity is simple, but it opens to us a book in which we never get beyond the first syllable.

Dag Hammarskjöld (174)

Holiness means the holiness of earthly, here-and-now life.

Joseph Soloveitchik (2, 33)

The politics of biblical spirituality involve the renunciation of worldly power and the condiments that commonly are associated with worldly power: wealth or the control thereof, success, fame, applause, ambition, avarice, goals, competitive esprit, and the rest of the success syndrome. Biblical spirituality means powerlessness, living without embellishment or pretense, free to be faithful in the gospel, and free from anxiety about effectiveness or similar illusions of success.

William Stringfellow (3, 44–45)

Holiness is the love of God at work in a concrete, active, deliberate way, which applies itself with rigour and precision to situations that are always fresh and always contemporary with the eternal love of God and with the human presence of men, women and children who are possessed with this love and, being contemporaneous with their epoch, express it in a way that only they can choose, discover and put into practice.

Anthony Bloom (3, 84–85)

All holiness is God's holiness in us: it is a holiness that is participation and, in a certain way, more than participation, because as we participate in what we can receive from God, we become a revelation of that which transcends us. Being a limited light, we reveal the Light.

Anthony Bloom (3, 93)

When I look at the galaxies on a clear night—when I look at the incredible brilliance of creation, and think that this is what God is like, then, instead of feeling intimidated and diminished by it, I am enlarged—I rejoice that I am part of it, I, you, all of us—part of this glory. And so, when we go to the altar to receive the bread and wine, we are taking into our bodies all of creation, all of the galaxies. And our total interdependence is an astounding glory.

Madeleine L'Engle (1, 82)

I do believe every soul has a tendency toward God.

Dorothy Day (12)

The only thing that can save the world from complete moral collapse is a spiritual revolution.

Thomas Merton (1, 3)

The need for spiritual liberation, the need for vision, the hunger and thirst for that perfect "justice" which is found in total surrender to God as love to the Beloved: these are the only real justifications for the monk's wilderness life and his desert pilgrimage.

Thomas Merton (4, 43)

The contemplative life must provide an area, a space of liberty, of silence, in which possibilities are allowed to surface and new choices—beyond routine choice—become manifest. It should create a new experience of time, not as stopgap, stillness, but as "temps vierge" [virginal time]—not a blank to be filled or an untouched space to be conquered and violated, but a space which can enjoy its own potentialities and hopes—and its own presence to itself. One's *own* time. But not dominated by one's own ego and its demands. Hence open to others—*compassionate* time, rooted in the sense of common illusion and in criticism of it.

Thomas Merton (2, 117)

And as to God, we must remember that the soul is but a hollow which God fills. Its union with God is, almost by definition, a continual self-abandonment—an opening, an unveiling, a surrender of itself. A blessed spirit is a mould ever more and more patient of the bright metal poured into it, a body ever more completely uncovered to the meridian blaze of the spiritual sun.

C. S. Lewis (4, 151)

The spiritual life has to do with the heart of existence. I find the word "heart" a good word. I don't mean by it the seat of our feelings as opposed to the seat of our thoughts. By "heart" I mean the centre of our being, the "place" where we are most ourselves, where we are most human, where we are most real. In that sense the heart is the focus of the spiritual life.

Henri Nouwen (3, 3–4)

The deep truth is that our human suffering need not be an obstacle to the joy and peace we so desire, but can become, instead, the means *to* it. The great secret of the spiritual life, the life of the Beloved Sons and Daughters of God, is that everything we live, be it gladness or sadness, joy or pain, health or illness, can all be part of the journey toward the full realization of our humanity.

Henri Nouwen (4, 77)

A spirituality of liberation must be filled with a living sense of *gratuitousness*. Communion with the Lord and with all men is more than anything else a gift. . . . This gift, far from being a call to passivity, demands a vigilant attitude. This is one of the most constant Biblical themes: the encounter with the Lord presupposes attention, active disposition, work, fidelity to his will, the good use of talents received.

Gustavo Gutiérrez (1, 205–6)

Living the spiritual life means living life as one unified reality. The forces of darkness are the forces that split, divide and set in opposition. The forces of light unite. Literally, the word "diabolic" means dividing. The demon divides; the Spirit unites.

The spiritual life counteracts the countless divisions that pervade our daily life and cause destruction and violence. These divisions are interior as well as exterior: the divisions among our most intimate emotions and the divisions among the most widespread social groupings. The division between gladness and sadness within me or the division between the races, religions and cultures around me all find their source in the diabolic forces of darkness. The Spirit of God, the Spirit that calls us the Beloved, is the Spirit that unites and makes whole. There is no clearer way to discern the presence of God's Spirit than to identify the moments of unification, healing, restoration and reconciliation. Wherever the Spirit works, divisions vanish and inner as well as outer unity manifests itself.

Henri Nouwen (4, 107–8)

Every human life, however humble, can do something to hasten or retard the triumph of the Eternal Charity. For God is not the God of the invisible creation alone. The new, the more real life that we expect must penetrate every level of existence and every relationship—politics, industry, science , art, our attitude to one another, our attitude to living nature—spiritualizing and unselfing all this; subduing it to the transforming action of "the intellectual radiance, full of love."

Evelyn Underhill (1, 102–3)

Parallel Scripture Passages

John 12:24–26	Galatians 4:1–7
2 Corinthians 5:14–16	John 6:63–66
Romans 6:3–11	Galatians 6:7–10
Colossians 3:10–11	Ezekiel 36:24–28
Colossians 2:1–17	1 Thessalonians 5:19–24
Galatians 5:16–26	

GLEANINGS

Justice and Kindness

The justice rendered to the Other, my neighbor, gives me an unsurpassable proximity to God. It is as intimate as the prayer and the liturgy which, without justice, are nothing. . . . *Justice* is the term Judaism prefers to terms more evocative of sentiment. For love itself demands justice, and my relation with my neighbor cannot remain outside the lines which this neighbor maintains with various third parties. The third party is also my neighbor.

Emmanuel Levinas (2, 18)

Be the living expression of God's kindness; kindness in your face, kindness in your eyes, kindness in your smile, kindness in your warm greeting. In the slums we are the light of God's kindness to the poor. To children, to the poor, to all who suffer and are lonely, give always a happy smile. Give them not only your care, but also your heart.

Mother Teresa of Calcutta (2, 44)

It is in *deeds* that man becomes aware of what his life really is, of his power to harm and to hurt, to wreck and to ruin; of his ability to derive joy and to bestow it upon others; to relieve and to increase his own and other people's tensions. . . . What he may not dare to think, he often utters in deeds. The heart is revealed in the deeds.

Abraham Heschel (284)

[A question to students:]
Are you going to prepare yourselves to dominate men, or to serve them?

Brother Roger (3, 106)

Christ Is José, Antonio, Severino

Let us press on without delay with the task of
    development
as a Christian means of evangelizing.
What value can there be in venerating pretty images of
    Christ,
or even recognizing his disfigured face in that of the poor,
if we fail to identify him with human beings
who need to be rescued from their underdeveloped
    condition.

However strange it may seem to some,
Christ in the North-East is called
José,
Antonio,
Severino . . .
Behold the man!
This is Christ,
the person who needs justice,
who has a right to justice,
who deserves justice.

Dom Helder Camara (2, 67–68)

Injustice anywhere is a threat to justice everywhere. We are caught in an
inescapable network of mutuality tied in a single garment of destiny.

Martin Luther King Jr. (2, 3)

Every time that there arises from the depths of a human heart the child-
ish cry which Christ himself could not restrain, "Why am I being hurt?"
then there is certainly injustice.

Simone Weil (6, 14)

To reduce Judaism to law, to *halacha,* is to dim its light, to pervert its
essence and to kill its spirit. We have a legacy of *agada* [moral teachings]
together with a system of *halacha,* . . . *halacha* is ultimately dependent
upon *agada.*

Abraham Heschel (338)

We must render kindness to acquire goodness; we must do the good to attain the holy.

Abraham Heschel (359)

To see a face is already to hear "You shall not kill", and to hear "you shall not kill" is to hear "Social justice".

Emmanuel Levinas (2, 8–9)

When God was merciful to us, we learned to be merciful with our brethren. When we received forgiveness instead of judgment, we, too, were made ready to forgive our brethren. What God did to us, we then owed to others. The more we received, the more we were able to give; and the more meager our brotherly love, the less were we living by God's mercy and love.

Dietrich Bonhoeffer (4, 24–25)

In a genuine dialogue each of the partners, even when he stands in opposition to the other, heeds, affirms, and confirms his opponent as an existing other. Only so can conflict certainly not be eliminated from the world but be humanly arbitrated and led toward its overcoming.

Martin Buber (1, 202)

Perhaps only a smile, a little visit, or simply the fact of building a fire for someone, writing a letter for a blind person, bringing a few coals, finding a pair of shoes, reading for someone, this is only a little bit, yes, a very tiny bit, but it will be our love of God in action.

Mother Teresa of Calcutta (1, 26)

Christ did not, like a moralist, love a theory of good, but He loved the real man. He was not, like a philosopher, interested in the "universally valid", but rather in that which is of help to the real and concrete human being.

Dietrich Bonhoeffer (2, 22)

To live in today's world and within it offer the solitary witness of staying unentangled, uncompromised by its power-struggles, unviolated by its attempts to corrupt is what will, in fact, change the world.

Maggie Ross (3, 107)

[Jesus] said: When you pray, use somewhat these words. Our father who are in the world and surpass the world. Blessed be your presence, in us, in animals and flowers, in still air and winds. May justice and peace dwell among us, as you come to us. Your will be our will; your will that we be brothers, as bread is bread, water is itself; for our hunger, for quenching of thirst. Forgive us. We walk crookedly in the world, are perverse, and fail of our promise. But we would be men, if only you consent to stir up our hearts. Amen.

Daniel Berrigan (1, 45)

[Some] good folk say . . . : "[Martin] Niemöller 'preached politics' too much, . . . instead of proclaiming the pure Gospel!" As if that would be the pure Gospel which did not imply a visible bodily life of the Church, which could ultimately remain completely invisible in the world!

Karl Barth (5, 72)

This I believe to be the privilege and the burden of all of us who deem ourselves bound by allegiances and loyalties which are broader and deeper than nationalism and which go beyond our nation's self-defined goals and positions. We are called to speak for the weak, for the voiceless, for victims of our nation and for those it calls enemy, for no document from human hands can make these humans any less our brothers.

Martin Luther King Jr. (1, 4)

[The community] speaks by the very fact of its existence in the world; by its characteristic attitude to world problems; and, moreover and especially, by its silent service to all the handicapped, weak, and needy in the world. It speaks, finally, by the simple fact that it prays for the world.

Karl Barth (4, 38)

That's what we're here for: to make the world new. We know what to do: seek justice, love mercy, walk humbly, treat every person as though she were yourself. These are not complicated instructions. It's much harder to decipher the directions for putting together a child's tricycle than it is to understand these.

Nancy Mairs (189)

How difficult it is to be just. We usually think of justice in terms of attribution or retribution, of allotting to everyone his due, but justice goes farther and claims more, much more, from us. It begins at the moment when I see my neighbour (individual or collective) as different from me, at times irreducibly different, and recognising his total right to be so, accept the fact that he is himself and has no reason to be merely a replica of myself. He is as much God's creature as I am; he was not made in my image but in God's.

Anthony Bloom (4, 48)

To acknowledge another man's right to be himself, not to resemble me, is the fundamental act of justice, which alone will make it possible for us to look at a man without trying to see and recognise ourselves in him, but to recognise him and beyond yet within him, to discern the Image of the Lord.

Anthony Bloom (4, 49)

We cannot love God unless we love each other, and to love we must know each other. We know Him in the breaking of bread, and we know each other in the breaking of bread, and we are not alone any more. Heaven is a banquet and life is a banquet, too, even with a crust, where there is companionship.

Dorothy Day (285)

I am telling you what Christianity is. I did not invent it. And there, right in the middle of it, I find "Forgive us our sins as we forgive those who sin against us." There is no slightest sign that we are offered forgiveness on any other terms. It is made perfectly clear that if we do not forgive we shall not be forgiven. There are no two ways about it.

C. S. Lewis (2, 104)

For if the soul itself, the person, was truly defenseless, forgiving, and loving, the result of this would be transparent minds, hearts and souls. A transparent soul would show *you* to everyone who seeks you, for unless we become transparent, people will not know you. For every human face is also the icon of Christ—so is every human heart.

Catherine de Hueck Doherty (163)

Parallel Scripture Passages

Luke 4:14–19   Psalm 82:1–4
Isaiah 1:11–20   Exodus 3:7–8
Isaiah 58:6–12   Jeremiah 22:13–16
Luke 14:12–14   Luke 3:10–14
Amos 5:2–24   Micah 6:6–8
Exodus 23:1–9

Love
of Neighbor

Love has a hem to her garment that reaches the very dust. It sweeps the stains from the streets and lanes, and because it can, it must.

Mother Teresa of Calcutta (1, 102)

To show great love for God and our neighbor we need not do great things. It is how much love we put in the doing that makes our offering Something Beautiful for God.

Mother Teresa of Calcutta (2, 69)

The love of God . . . is a commandment to love. . . . One can command love, but it is love that commands love, and it commands it in the *now* of its love, in such a way that the commandment to love is repeated and renewed indefinitely in the repetition and renewal of the very love that commands love.

Emmanuel Levinas (2, 191)

The Revelation of God to Man, which is the love of God for Man, provokes Man's response. Man's response to God's love is the love of one's neighbor. God's Revelation therefore begins the work of Redemption which is none the less Man's own work.

Emmanuel Levinas (2, 192)

Because we cannot see Christ, we cannot express our love to Him in person. But our neighbor we can see, and we can do for him or her what we would love to do for Jesus if He were visible. Let us open to God so that He can use us. Let us put love into our actions, beginning in the family, in the neighborhood, in the street. It is difficult, but there is where the work begins. We are co-workers of Christ, a fruitbearing branch of the vine.

Mother Teresa of Calcutta (1, 17)

The man who sees someone in affliction and projects into him his own being brings to birth in him through love, at least for a moment, an existence apart from his affliction.

Simone Weil (5, 190)

Is morality possible without God? I answer with a question: is divinity possible without relation to a human Other? . . . As Jews, we are always a threesome: I and you and the Third who is in our midst. And only as a Third does He reveal Himself.

Emmanuel Levinas (1, 247)

The essential human reality is no longer to be regarded as one of the individual life (even as little as one of the collective life), but as something that takes place between man and man, between I and Thou.

Martin Buber (1, 94)

In the nearness and love of another it [humanity] comes to know its home; in its alienness and unworthiness it knows the alienness of the world; in the mystery of the "I," it first encounters the mystery of self. In short, in the experience of the other it experiences everything that it means to be human. . . .

Face-to-face with the existence of his neighbor, he first experiences that primordial "responsibility for everything" and thus becomes a special creature capable of fellow feeling with a complete stranger, of loving even that which he does not erotically desire or on whom he is not dependent for his existence-in-the-world.

Václav Havel (1, 370)

Charity, the beginning and the end of all spiritual relationships. Christian charity, which is preached so fervently by the Gospels, is nothing else than the more or less conscious cohesion of souls engendered by their communal convergence *in Christo Jesu*. It is impossible to love Christ without loving others (in proportion as these others are moving towards Christ). And it is impossible to love others (in a spirit of broad human communion) without moving nearer to Christ.

Pierre Teilhard de Chardin (1, 144)

[Nonviolent love] is the abolition of barriers and limits, perpetual giving without loss, total sacrifice without suffering, and thus makes our nature the same as the nature of light. It is the only door into the Kingdom, for God is truth and truth is the goal, but love is the way. That is why love of God which does not show itself through service to mankind is a snare and a delusion.

Lanza del Vasto (3, 115)

God became not only a man, but Man. This is the mystery of the Redemption and our salvation is worked out on earth according as we love one another, see Christ in one another, etc., by works. This is one reason I am chary of using the word, love, loosely. I prefer to use it in its practical forms, such as prayer, almsgiving, visiting the sick and burying the dead and so forth.

Flannery O'Connor (1, 102)

Conceiving love only as a warm fuzzy, you can readily forget just how much work it entails. But it's authentic work, strenuous and productive: doing a do, not avoiding a don't. It puts you in a right relation with God and others, reciprocal rather than hierarchical. At one time or another, legal penalties have been imposed for violations of all the ten commandments. . . . But the great commandment is extralegal. Love cannot be forced. It must be chosen. You love not out of dread but out of your own fullness. It's what you were made for. When you fail at it, you aren't sent to prison, or to the electric chair, or to hell. You are commanded again: Love.

Nancy Mairs (139)

When you have reached the point where you no longer expect a response, you will at least be able to give in such a way that the other is able to receive, and be grateful. When Love has matured and, through a dissolution of the self into light, become a radiance, then shall the Lover be liberated from dependence upon the Beloved, and the Beloved also be made perfect by being liberated from the Lover.

Dag Hammarskjöld (76)

It is not a simple thing to accept God's love, because if we do, we must return love.

Madeleine L'Engle (5, 76)

A Russian priest, Father Anthony, told me, "To say to anyone 'I love you' is tantamount to saying 'You shall live forever.' "

I am slowly beginning to learn something about immortality.

Madeleine L'Engle (2, 110)

"Who is my neighbor?" The neighbor was the Samaritan who *approached* the wounded man and *made him his neighbor.* The neighbor . . . is not he whom I find in my path, but rather he in whose path I place myself, he whom I approach and actively seek.

Gustavo Gutiérrez (1, 198)

"Who is my neighbour?" . . . The answer is: "You are the neighbour. Go along and try to be obedient by loving others." Neighbourliness is not a quality in other people, it is simply their claim on ourselves. Every moment and every situation challenges us to action and to obedience.

Dietrich Bonhoeffer (1, 67)

In the first legend of the Grail, it is said that the Grail (the miraculous vessel that satisfies all hunger by virtue of the consecrated Host) belongs to the first comer who asks the guardian of the vessel, a king three-quarters paralyzed by the most painful wound, "What are you going through?"

The love of our neighbor in all of its fullness simply means being able to say to him: "What are you going through?" It is a recognition that the sufferer exists, not only as a unit in a collection, or a specimen from the social category labeled "unfortunate," but as a man, exactly like us, who was one day stamped with a special mark by affliction. For this reason it is enough, but it is indispensable, to know how to look at him in a certain way.

This way of looking is first of all attentive. The soul empties itself of all its own contents in order to receive into itself the being it is looking at, just as he is, in all his truth.

Only he who is capable of attention can do this.

Simone Weil (7, 115)

Love, of course, means something much more than mere sentiment, much more than token favours and perfunctory almsdeeds. Love means an interior and spiritual identification with one's brother, so that he is not regarded as an "object" to "which" one "does good." The fact is that good done to another as to an object is of little or no spiritual value. Love takes one's neighbour as one's other self, and loves him with all the immense humility and discretion and reserve and reverence without which no one can presume to enter into the sanctuary of another's subjectivity. From such love all authoritarian brutality, all exploitation, domineering and condescension must necessarily be absent.

Thomas Merton (8, 17–18)

It is love that will make me forgive always and every time! So I began to meditate on the power of love. Once again I experienced a return to the Holy Land, where I had an encounter with Christ.

Catherine de Hueck Doherty (155–56)

I tried to understand. Suddenly I discovered the things that were more important than bread, things that we can give to one another: faith in God, trust in one another, love, hope. This is the true almsgiving that men must give to each other today.

Catherine de Hueck Doherty (188)

When we have found our own uniqueness in the love of God and have been able to affirm that indeed we are lovable since it is God's love that dwells in us, then we can reach out to others in whom we discover a new and unique manifestation of the same love and enter into an intimate communion with them.

Henri Nouwen (1, 68)

Jesus shows us that true love, the love that comes from God, makes no distinction between friends and foes, between people who are for us and people who are against us, people who do us a favour and people who do us ill. God makes no such distinction. He loves all human beings, good or bad, with the same unconditional love. This all-embracing love Jesus offers to us, and he invites us to make this love visible in our lives.

Henri Nouwen (3, 54)

When I speak of love I am not speaking of some sentimental and weak response. I am speaking of that force which all of the great religions have seen as the supreme unifying principle of life. Love is somehow the key that unlocks the door which leads to ultimate reality. This Hindu–Moslem–Christian–Jewish–Buddhist belief about ultimate reality is beautifully summed up in the first epistle of Saint John: "Let us love one another; for love is God and everyone that loveth is born of God and knoweth God. He that loveth not knoweth not God; for God is love. If we love one another, God dwelleth in us, and his love is perfected in us."

Let us hope that this spirit will become the order of the day.

Martin Luther King Jr. (1, 10)

One of the most rewarding aspects of living in a strange land is the experience of being loved not for what we can do, but for who we are. When we become aware that our stuttering, failing, vulnerable selves are loved even when we hardly progress, we can let go of our compulsion to prove ourselves and be free to live with others in a fellowship of the weak. That is true healing.

Henri Nouwen (2, 17)

Parallel Scripture Passages

John 13:34–35	Luke 10:25–37
John 15:12–17	1 John 4:16–21
Romans 12:9–18	1 Peter 3:8–12
1 Corinthians 13:4–7	James 2:1–8
Ephesians 5:1–2	

GLEANINGS

Peace and Peacemaking

Make of me a rainbow . . .

. . . of kindness,
hope,
and peace! . . .
A rainbow
that will never lie—
never proclaim false kindness,
vain hope,
mendacious peace . . .
A rainbow spread by you,
presage and promise
that these will never fail:
   your Fatherly Love,
   the Death of your Son,
   and the prodigious Action
      of your Spirit, Lord!

Dom Helder Camara (2, 53)

What God wills for man is a helpful, healing, and uplifting work, and what he does with him brings peace and joy.

Karl Barth (4, 11)

Who has seen the same dawn twice? Who has seen the same sunset twice?

Dom Helder Camara (3, 23)

How could we be filled with hatred, if we live night and day in God who is love?

Dom Helder Camara (3, 24)

> Lord Jesus, at your arrest,
> when your companion
> put his hand on his sword,
> drew it,
> struck the servant on the ear
> and cut it off,
> you said to him:
> "Put your sword back in its scabbard,
> for all
> who take the sword
> will perish by the sword."
> What do you say
> to the making and use
> of nuclear arms?

Dom Helder Camara (1, 39)

Darkness, chaos, death, and hell may be noted, but never for a moment do they gain the upper hand. As Mozart makes music, he knows all this from some mysterious center, and he thus observes the limits both right and left, both above and below. He maintains due proportion. . . . There is in his music no light that does not also know shadow, no joy that does not include pain, but also no terror, anger, or complaint that peace does not accompany either closely or at a distance. No laughter without tears, but also no tears without laughter . . . ! In Mozart's music the true voice of humanity comes to expression. . . . Those who hear it aright . . . understand themselves as the people they are . . . as those who have fallen victim to death but who still live, and they feel themselves summoned to freedom.

Karl Barth (7, 94–95)

Lord . . . do not let us fall either today or tomorrow. Free us from all tension or mere routine, from the tyranny of custom, fashion, and public opinion. Let us hear thy word, and give us the courage and freedom to pray to thee. And so convert us continually to thanksgiving in heart and deed, that we may not perish but have everlasting life.

Karl Barth (7, 96–97)

I remember a man of some standing who once came to see me and told me that a friend of his who claimed no small spiritual achievements had offended him: "Who should go and make his peace with the other?" he asked. "I cannot answer your question," I replied, "as I cannot possibly set myself as a judge between you, but one thing is certain to me: the meanest of the two of you will wait for the other to make the move." The great man said no word, but went forthwith to make his peace with his friend.

Anthony Bloom (4, 107)

If you dislike war, respect your neighbor.
And cherish the man who comes from afar.
Venerate the distance in him.
Distance is like an allusion to the infinite.
Love the man in your neighbor.
Love God in the man who comes from afar.

Lanza del Vasto (2, 141)

My study of Gandhi convinced me that true pacifism is not nonresistance to evil, but nonviolent resistance to evil. Between the two positions, there is a world of difference. Gandhi resisted evil with as much vigor and power as the violent resister, but he resisted with love instead of hate. True pacifism is not unrealistic submission to evil power, as [Reinhold] Niebuhr contends. It is rather a courageous confrontation of evil by the power of love, in the faith that it is better to be the recipient of violence than the inflicter of it, since the latter only multiplies the existence of violence and bitterness in the universe, while the former may develop a sense of shame in the opponent, and thereby bring about a transformation and change of heart.

Martin Luther King Jr. (3, 8)

The Bible teaches in many places, warns, illustrates, denounces, illumines this bitter truth: the violence of humans is in essence genocidal, mass suicidal. War is not itself until it is total war, laying claim to the total person, the human family in toto, universal life. Such a will, in our lifetime, creates weapons to match its madness; and for once, the weapons are equal to the will. They are merciless as ourselves, they at length resemble us, our alter ego. War has thus become the ultimate anti-Christ, the obscene god of death, condemning all life to capital punishment.

Daniel Berrigan (2, 116)

War effaces all conceptions of purpose or goal, including even its own "war aims." It effaces the very notion of war's being brought to an end. To be outside a situation so violent as this is to find it inconceivable; to be inside it is to be unable to conceive its end. Consequently, nobody does anything to bring this end about. In the presence of an armed enemy, what hand can relinquish its weapon? The mind ought to find a way out, but the mind has lost all capacity to so much as look outward. The mind is completely absorbed in doing itself violence. Always in human life, whether war or slavery is in question, intolerable sufferings continue, as it were, by the force of their own specific gravity.

Simone Weil (3, 22)

One must possess power in order to renounce it. One must possess courage in order to renounce violence. One must show one's courage by refusing to be violent.

Lanza del Vasto (3, 118)

Violence obliterates anybody who feels its touch.

Simone Weil (3, 19)

Peacemaking is a work of love, and love casts out fear. "In love there can be no fear, but fear is driven out by perfect love" (1 John 18). Nothing is more important in peacemaking than that it flows from a deep and undeniable experience of love. Only those who deeply know that they are loved and rejoice in that love can be true peacemakers, because the intimate knowledge of being loved sets us free to look beyond the boundaries of death and to speak and act fearlessly for peace.

Henri Nouwen (10, 6)

As peacemakers we must resist resolutely all the powers of war and destruction and proclaim that peace is the divine gift offered to all who affirm life.

Henri Nouwen (10, 7)

Only he who has measured the dominion of force, and knows how not to respect it, is capable of love and justice.

Simone Weil (3, 34)

Parallel Scripture Passages

Luke 19:41–42	Ephesians 4:25–32	James 3:13–18
Matthew 5:43–48	John 14:27–29	Ephesians 2:11–16
1 John 2:3–11	John 16:25–33	2 Corinthians 5:16–20
Matthew 5:23–26	Isaiah 9:5–6	Matthew 5:9
Isaiah 2:2–5		

Prayer and Work

Prayer, which is called in Hebrew "the service of the heart" or even "the work of the heart" (once again, such an expression is not simply a metaphor) refers, in the true sense of the term, to the task of edifying the worlds, or "repairing the ruins of creation." For the self (*moi*), prayer means that, instead of seeking one's own salvation, one secures that of others.

Emmanuel Levinas (1, 233)

Perhaps, if we walk with God our sense of wonder is untouched, we retain our joy at being simply who we are, faulted and flawed, but God's. Perhaps if we walk with God, our lives are truly nothing but prayer.

Madeleine L'Engle (1, 106)

Prayer is basically an awareness of man finding himself in the presence of and addressing himself to his Maker, and to pray has one connotation only: to stand before God. . . . It remains unalterably true that the very essence of prayer is the covenantal experience of being together with and talking to God and that the concrete performance such as the recitation of texts represents the technique of implementation of prayer and not prayer itself.

Joseph Soloveitchik (1, 56–57)

Every prayer has its beginning when a man puts himself (together with his best and most accomplished work) out of the picture. He leaves himself and his work behind in order once again to recollect that he stands before God.

Karl Barth (4, 162)

If in your morning prayers you have said a phrase, you must live up to this phrase in the course of the day. . . . You must make a rule that when you have discovered one phrase which makes sense to you—in the reading of the Gospel, in the reading of the New or Old Testament in general, in praying with words from the liturgy—you must try to apply it in the course of the day ruthlessly, for as long as you can. . . . If you can keep to one sentence of one prayer for an hour without breaking the rule you will be lucky, but do it!

Anthony Bloom (1, 59)

Work. Prayer. As with all of life, it is a rhythm: tension, release; tension, release. Work, discipline, obedience; pull the bow string taut, and then let go. But it must be done daily.

Madeleine L'Engle (6, 150)

The resistance to praying is like the resistance of tightly clenched fists.

Henri Nouwen (12, 12)

To pray means to open your hands before God. It means slowly relaxing the tension which squeezes your hands together and accepting your existence with an increasing readiness, not as a possession to defend, but as a gift to receive. Above all, therefore, prayer is a way of life which allows you to find a stillness in the midst of the world where you open your hands to God's promises, and find hope for yourself, your fellowman and the whole community in which you live. In prayer, you encounter God in the soft breeze, in the distress and joy of your neighbor and in the loneliness of your own heart.

Henri Nouwen (12, 154)

A few moments of the day can be salvaged for God, yes, but the best hours are absorbed, or at any rate cheapened by material cares.

Pierre Teilhard de Chardin (1, 65)

Love prayer. Feel often the need to pray, and take the trouble to pray. It is by praying often that you will pray better. Prayer enlarges the heart until it is capable of containing the gift that God makes of Himself. Ask and seek: your heart will grow capable of receiving Him and holding on to Him.

Mother Teresa of Calcutta (1, 7)

In prayer, theological work is the inner, spiritual, and vertically directed motion of man; while in study, although similarly external, it runs in a horizontal direction.

Karl Barth (4, 171)

We have to pray where we are, and what we can. And we shouldn't try to fool ourselves; intercession is hard work. We are lazy about it and avoid it for very good reasons. Prayer, especially intercession, is warfare. Prayer is death. As we pray we fast; as we pray we die. We have to deny ourselves everything else that is in our lives and just *do* it.

Maggie Ross (1, 109)

The spiritual life and the life of prayer always grow into greater simplicity, and it is important that each person should consciously encourage this tendency by seeking simplicity and purity in life as in prayer. It is always appropriate to yield to moments of silence in prayer, to be silent in order to let God speak if he will.

A Carthusian (92)

Unless the prayer which you intend to offer to God is important and meaningful to you first, you will not be able to present it to the Lord. If you are inattentive to the words you pronounce, if your heart does not respond to them, or if your life is not turned to the same direction as your prayer, it will not reach out Godwards.

Anthony Bloom (2, 26)

We never pray alone. Ever. Even if there is no other human being around us who is willing or able to pray with us, we are in the company of angels and archangels. And, even when we feel most isolated, there *are* other human creatures, somewhere, who are praying with us.

Madeleine L'Engle (1, 56)

We begin our day by seeing Christ in the consecrated bread, and throughout the day we continue to see Him in the torn bodies of our poor. We pray, that is, through our work, performing it with Jesus, for Jesus, and upon Jesus. The poor are our prayer. They carry God in them.

Mother Teresa of Calcutta (1, 8)

In prayer, in the creative process, these two parts of ourselves, the mind and the heart, the intellect and the intuition, the conscious and the subconscious mind, stop fighting each other and collaborate.

Madeleine L'Engle (6, 162)

Prayer in its primal and fundamental sense . . . means *a radical response to life*.

Matthew Fox (1, 49)

The work of the hands is indeed the apprenticeship to honesty.

Honesty is a certain equality one establishes between what one takes and what one gives.

Lanza del Vasto (3, 103)

Let the work of your hands be an act of gratitude for the human state and homage to it. One stoops in order to bow: bow to every man by stooping to work.

Lanza del Vasto (3, 104)

I cannot pray if I don't serve my brother. I cannot pray to the God who incarnated himself when my brother is in need. It is an impossibility. It would be like the priest, the Levite, who passed the man beset by robbers, and that one cannot do.

Catherine de Hueck Doherty (45)

I am impatient, restless, full of preoccupations, and easily suspicious. Maybe I just need to repeat this sentence very often and let it sink deep into my heart: "By waiting and calm, you shall be saved. In quiet and trust lies your strength." (Isa. 30:15) If these words could descend from my head into my heart and become part of my innermost self, I would be a converted man. "Lord Jesus Christ, Son of the Living God, have mercy on me, a sinner."[3]

Henri Nouwen (1, 16)

Perhaps the challenge of the gospel lies precisely in the invitation to accept a gift for which we can give nothing in return. For the gift is the life breath of God himself, the Spirit who is poured out on us through Jesus Christ. This life breath frees us from fear and gives us new room to live. A man who prayerfully goes about his life is constantly ready to receive the breath of God, and to let his life be renewed and expanded. The man who never prays, on the contrary, is like the child with asthma; because he is short of breath, the whole world shrivels up before him. He creeps in a corner gasping for air, and is virtually in agony. But the man who prays opens himself to God and can freely breathe again. He stands upright, stretches out his hands and comes out of his corner, free to boldly stride through the world because he can move about without fear.

A man who prays is one who can once more breathe freely, who has the freedom to move where he wishes with no fears to haunt him.

Henri Nouwen (12, 64)

The prayer of the heart requires first of all that we make God our only thought. That means that we must dispel all distractions, concerns, worries and preoccupations, and fill the mind with God alone. The Jesus prayer, or any other prayer form, is meant to be a help to gently empty our minds from all that is not God, and offer all the room to him and him alone. But that is not all. Our prayer becomes a prayer of the heart when we have localized in the center of our inner being the empty space in which our God-filled mind can descend and vanish, and where the distinctions between thinking and feeling, knowing and experiencing, ideas and emotions are transcended and where God can become our host.

Henri Nouwen (8, 105–6)

To the degree that our prayer has become the prayer of our heart we will love more and suffer more, we will see more light and more darkness, more grace and more sin, more of God and more of humanity. To the degree that we have descended into our heart and reached out to God from there, solitude can speak to solitude, deep to deep and heart to heart. It is there where love and pain are found together.

Henri Nouwen (8, 107–8)

Real prayer is a mutual act. It is that correspondence between our dependent spirits and His Absolute Spirit, worked partly by grace, but also partly by our wills which is our mysterious privilege as living children of the Spirit of all spirits, God. This deep communion, this "prayer which is ceaseless," continues without interruption in the ground of the loving soul.

Evelyn Underhill (1, 145)

The most promising method of prayer is to allow oneself to be guided by the word of the Scriptures, to pray on the basis of a word of Scripture. In this way we shall not become the victims of our own emptiness. Prayer means nothing else but the readiness and willingness to receive and appropriate the Word.

Dietrich Bonhoeffer (4, 84)

Parallel Scripture Passages

Luke 11:5–13	Psalm 143:1	Colossians 3:23–24
Matthew 6:5–8	1 Timothy 2:1–8	John 15:1–10
1 John 5:14–15	Luke 6:12	Romans 8:26–27
Matthew 6:7–14	Matthew 26:36–44	James 5:13–20

GLEANINGS

Purity of Heart: Humility and Renunciation

Be grateful as your deeds become less and less associated with your name, as your feet ever more lightly tread the earth.

Dag Hammarskjöld (146)

Human truth, both Christian and Jewish, is verification. It consists in risking one's life by living it in reply to the Revelation—that is to say, in reply to the Love of God.

Emmanuel Levinas (2, 195)

Humility is above all one of the qualities of attention.

Simone Weil (1, 351)

It is part of the discipline of humility that we must not spare our hand where it can perform a service and that we do not assume that our schedule is our own to manage, but allow it to be arranged by God.

Dietrich Bonhoeffer (4, 99)

In God you come up against something which is in every respect immeasurably superior to yourself. Unless you know God as that—and, therefore, know yourself as nothing in comparison—you do not know God at all. As long as you are proud you cannot know God. A proud man is always looking down on things and people: and, of course, as you are looking down, you cannot see something that is above you.

C. S. Lewis (2, 111)

Purity of heart can only be lived in spontaneous and joyous forgetfulness of self in order to lay down one's life for those one loves.

Brother Roger (1, 87)

To be a saint does not mean never to sin. It means to start again with humility and joy after each fall.

Dom Helder Camara (3, 27)

But to love in all things, we must love you beyond all things; to be true to the earth, we must be true to you, Father in heaven. Otherwise our love becomes a tragic convulsion and ends in lies and self-rebellion. For this reason, may your Spirit teach us to give up all things for your sake; not to let them go packing, but to release them to you, with an impulse of love as it were, which releases them and lets them roll on your track. If it is an impulse of love, then they take our love along with them and we have provided ourselves a rendezvous with you.

Hans Urs von Balthasar (430)

It is true that humility is not a virtue one can set about acquiring. It is a grace that descends on the best of us. Make yourself worthy to receive it.

Lanza del Vasto (3, 104)

Purity of heart is purity of love. We are pure in the measure that we love. Love is always pure. Because God is love, love is purity itself. Everything that springs from love is good and holy.

A Carthusian (44)

My very uniqueness lies in my responsibility for the other; nobody can relieve me of this, just as nobody can replace me at the moment of my death. Obedience to the Most High is defined for me by precisely this impossibility of running away; through this, my "self" is unique. To be free is simply to do what nobody else can do in my place. To obey the Most High is to be free.

Emmanuel Levinas (1, 202)

[Marking his sixtieth birthday, Teilhard writes:]

My whole spiritual life consists more and more in abandoning myself (actively) to the presence and action of God. To be in communion with Becoming has become the formula of my whole life.

Pierre Teilhard de Chardin (2, 283)

Goodness is something so simple: always to live for others, never to seek one's own advantage.

Dag Hammarskjöld (89)

> Prayer for Friday:
> Lord, be my bread today,
> the spring of my strength,
> my hunger, my thirst, my desire, my joy.
> Keep me from the loves that are not
> love of Thee.
> Deliver me from my nature, Lord,
> and take my place in me.

Lanza del Vasto (2, 50)

Religion begins with a consciousness that something is asked of us.

Abraham Heschel (162)

The spirit of poverty does not consist in pursuing misery, but in setting everything in the simple beauty of creation.

The spirit of poverty is to live in the gladness of today.

Brother Roger (1, 93)

To be without desire is a mark of poverty. At the moment I am surrounded by people who cling to their desires, so much so that they haven't any interest for others: they give up listening, and are incapable of loving their neighbour.

Dietrich Bonhoeffer (3, 148)

Fasting is not confined to restricting our intake of food. Fasting is not a diet any more than solitude is the same as living alone. Any time we say "no" to ourselves we fast, whether in a sudden surge of resolve to stop being seduced by a particularly fashionable act of immorality, or, at the opposite end of the spectrum, to give up a good option in order to make ourselves available for something of even greater value.

In conscious still prayer we gently eliminate everything else in our lives: activities, thoughts, distractions.

Maggie Ross (1, 34)

When the great experience of the overwhelming love that God has for us came to St. Teresa, she was struck to her knees, weeping in joy and wonder; when she arose she was a new person, one in whom the realisation of God's love left her "with a sense of unpayable debt". This is humility—not humiliation. . . . One's humble state is not abasement but simply remaining before God in wonder, joy and gratitude.

Anthony Bloom (4, 68–69)

Before we can surrender ourselves we must become ourselves. For no one can give up what he does not possess.

Thomas Merton (9, 31)

We make a terrible error when we think that to be human means to be perfect, some kind of unerring Christian model that cannot exist in reality. Only God is perfect. To be human is to be able to laugh, to cry, to live fully, to be aware of our lives as we are living them.

Madeleine L'Engle (4, 158)

Our seeking of God is not all a matter of our finding him by means of certain ascetic techniques. It is rather a quieting and ordering of our whole life by self-denial, prayer, and good works, so that God himself, who seeks us more than we seek him, can "find us" and "take possession of us."

Thomas Merton (5, 29)

Once I have decided to put my will into the immense sea of Christ's will, I seem to come to a moment of nonexistence, and there are no ways in which I can put it into words. It is as if by total surrender of my will I also surrender my body, my mind, my senses, everything that is me, and I am as if I were not.

Catherine de Hueck Doherty (125)

Parallel Scripture Passages

Psalm 24:1–6	Luke 14:25–33	Luke 22:24–27
Matthew 5:8	Matthew 6:19–21	Matthew 23:1–12
Luke 18:18–25	Matthew 6:24	Luke 17:7–10
Luke 9:23–27	Luke 9:46–48	John 13:1–20
Luke 14:7–11	Matthew 20:24–28	

GLEANINGS

Scripture and Sacred Texts

The Bible is an answer to the question: how to sanctify life.

Abraham Heschel (237)

The Bible . . . continues to scatter seeds of justice and compassion, to echo God's cry to the world and to pierce man's armor of callousness.

Abraham Heschel (239)

There is, simply, no reason to presuppose that *anyone* will find the gospel, as such, likable. . . .
. . . "Bless those who persecute you, bless and do not curse them" (Rom. 12:14).

William Stringfellow (2, 110)

Biblical words are like musical signs of a divine harmony which only the finest chords of the soul can utter. It is the sense of the holy that perceives the presence of God in the Bible.

Abraham Heschel (252)

The Bible is the book of the Promise, the Promise made by God to men which is the efficacious revelation of his love and his self-communication; simultaneously it reveals man to himself.

Gustavo Gutiérrez (1, 160)

The Bible is a seed, God is the sun, but we are the soil. Every generation is expected to bring forth new understanding and new realization.

Abraham Heschel (274)

The Gospel is accessible to all. One can hear it any day at any hour of the day, and it seems childishly clear and simple. But which of us is child enough to understand it? It shines out like a lighted candle, but only those who have eyes to see can see. And however much it is read and preached, its meaning, like the meaning of every living thing, guards itself from those who have no ears to hear.

Lanza del Vasto (1, 16–17)

The Gospel contains a conception of human life, not a theology.

Simone Weil (1, 147)

Proper reading of Scripture is not a technical exercise that can be learned; it is something that grows or diminishes according to one's own spiritual frame of mind. The crude, ponderous rendition of the Bible by many a Christian grown old in experience often far surpasses the most highly polished reading of a minister.

Dietrich Bonhoeffer (4, 56–57)

To those who read Scripture in an academic or aesthetic or merely devotional way the Bible indeed offers pleasant refreshment and profitable thoughts. But to learn the inner secrets of the Scripture we must make them our true daily bread, find God in them when we are in greatest need—and usually when we can find Him nowhere else and have nowhere else to look!

Thomas Merton (9, 117)

There is, simply, this danger in reading the Bible that one may be emancipated from the jargon, stereotypes, fables and similar encumbrances of church tradition and hear the Word of God. Well, I was being (I am being) regularly devastated in the privacy of my encounter with the biblical Word and that kept challenging the propriety of my ecclesiastical activities.

William Stringfellow (4, 144)

Scriptures . . . establish a connection between generations; . . . they must guarantee the connection between the center and the periphery of the community.

Franz Rosenzweig (275)

Biblically speaking, healing is never accomplished by the powerful, by those in command. Indeed the Bible underscores the illness of wrong power, the spirit of control, of ego run amok.

The conditions of these so afflicted were, but for the compassion of God, all but terminal.

Daniel Berrigan (4, 230)

In time, his [God's] preferences grow reasonably clear, consistent. They grow more than clear in the case of Jesus—blindingly self-evident. This young rabbi claims a privileged place in the line of prophets. He steps calmly into that place and promptly pays for it with his blood. And God, the great Absenter, Abstainer, albeit tardily, is with him; in a stupendous intervention, the dead man walks again.

Daniel Berrigan (3, 67)

The message of the Bible is then that into the confusion of man's world, with its divisions and hatred, has come a message of transforming power, and those who believe it will experience in themselves the love that makes for reconciliation and peace on earth.

Thomas Merton (7, 21–22)

We must not forget that the word of God issues its challenges. The scriptures are not a passive store of answers to our questions. We indeed read the Bible, but we can also say that the Bible "reads us." In many instances, our very questions will be reformulated. In the gospels this happens frequently to those who approach Jesus. For example, when Jesus is asked: "Who is my neighbor?" he reverses the terms of the question and inquires in turn: Which of these three . . . proved neighbor to the man?" (Luke 10:29, 36).

Gustavo Gutiérrez (2, 34)

The psalms rehearse every need, every desire, every complaint, every appeal, every mood, every experience of every sort, and thus one turns to the psalms to be prompted or inspired, edified or prodded, reminded or consoled. And that represents enough spiritual exercise for anyone.

William Stringfellow (3, 24)

To say that the Bible goes beyond religion is to say that it preaches the *kenosis* or self-emptying of God and his identification of himself with man as person and as community, in Christ.

Thomas Merton (7, 86)

[The biblical message] speaks about the One who . . . , from the very outset is the Neighbor, Companion and Brother of every man.

Karl Barth (2, 134)

Biblically, the Holy Spirit means the militant presence of the Word of God inhering in the life of the whole of creation. Biblically, the Holy Spirit is the Word of God at work both historically and existentially, acting incessantly and pervasively to renew the integrity of life in this world.

William Stringfellow (3, 18)

Parallel Scripture Passages

Luke 24:13–35
Luke 4:14–21
2 Timothy 3:10–17

Silence and Solitude

I was very surprised at the benefit I immediately gained from [taking up silence]. It enabled me to gauge how much we unwittingly lose by dispersing ourselves, how much of our substance a futile word carries away. The silence of the mouth gains thought and the heart. Inner life takes a peaceful turn and gravitates more freely. Things and people are seen as through a glass. We draw back; go up a flight; the hollow we have created resounds.

Lanza del Vasto (3, 228)

Do not flee to solitude from the community. Find God first in the community, then He will lead you to solitude.

Thomas Merton (9, 110)

Sometimes solitude is like a balancing on the edge of a razor blade, with a meadow full of wildflowers on one hand, and madness on the other.

Or, solitude is like a tea ceremony, the celebration of life in all its homely movements taken out of time. The wonder of the commonplace; the mystery of ordinary life: eating, sleeping, reading, listening to God's secrets and jokes, a sense of delight, of dance, of coming to fruition, learning that solitude is not something we need to scramble to fill up, but that it is full and overflowing if we can learn to accept the familiarity of insecurity and let go.

Maggie Ross (1, 139)

In eternity the spoken word fades away into the silence of perfect togetherness—for union occurs in silence only; the word unites, but those who are united fall silent. And so liturgy, the reflector which focuses the sunbeams of eternity in the small circle of the year, must introduce man to this silence. But even in liturgy, shared silence can come only at the end, and all that goes before is a preparation for this end. In the stage of preparation the word still dominates the scene. The word itself must take man to the point of learning how to share silence. His preparation begins with learning to hear.

Franz Rosenzweig (307)

Let him who cannot be alone beware of community. He will only do harm to himself and to the community. Alone you stood before God when he called you; alone you had to answer that call; alone you had to struggle and pray; and alone you will die and give an account to God. You cannot escape from yourself; for God has singled you out. If you refuse to be alone you are rejecting Christ's call to you, and you can have no part in the community of those who are called. . . .

But the reverse is also true: *Let him who is not in community beware of being alone.*

Dietrich Bonhoeffer (4, 77)

Solitude precludes the empire building that attaches to property, physical or mental (yours or someone else's); solitude rules our security and physical stability that rely on legal agreements, which, if you're poor, will invariably lead to exploitation.

Solitude is disengagement from human power struggles in order to have the detachment and clear-sightedness to undertake true political action with integrity. Solitude is living simply and, for the likes of me, singly, through doing for yourself as opposed to having an elaborate network of people to support an artificial enclosure and an artificial image.

Solitude seeks the humility of vulnerability.

Maggie Ross (4, 126)

Every deed and every relationship is surrounded by an atmosphere of silence. Friendship needs no words—it is solitude delivered from the anguish of loneliness.

Dag Hammarskjöld (8)

To preserve the silence within—amid all the noise. To remain open and quiet, a moist humus in the fertile darkness where the rain falls and the grain ripens—no matter how many tramp across the parade ground in whirling dust under an arid sky.

Dag Hammarskjöld (83)

Be silent much in order to have something to say worth hearing. But again be silent to hear yourself.

Lanza del Vasto (2, 52)

If our life is poured out in useless words, we will never hear anything, will never become anything, and in the end, because we have said everything before we had anything to say we shall be left speechless at the moment of our greatest decision.

Thomas Merton (9, 88)

How grateful we can be in such a world for words which issue out of silence! Silence, the spirit, the fountainhead, eternally self-renewing, giving but never spent, austere but warm of heart, insistent, self-judging, the companion and interpreter of dreams and deeds alike! I remember during the sixties, urging social activists to spend a half hour of silence for every two hours they spent in talk. I have no evidence the advice was heeded. But to me "pure activism" is pure insanity, impossible in fact, a violation of our being, a social monstrosity. . . .

What place is silence accorded here and now?

Daniel Berrigan (3, 13)

No one can take you into the desert. You must find the path yourself. Plunge into your loneliness, your hunger, your thirst. In the desert you will be purified and tempted; God will speak to your heart and angels will come and minister to you.

Maggie Ross (1, 142)

[We can be happy] if we learn a certain amount of silence. Begin with the silence of the lips, with the silence of the emotions, the silence of the mind, the silence of the body. . . . We must start by silencing our lips, by silencing our body in the sense of learning to keep still, to let tenseness go, not to fall into day-dreaming and slackness. . . . And from then on-wards we must learn to listen to silence, to be absolutely quiet, and we may, more often than we imagine, discover that the words of the Book of Revelation come true: "I stand at the door and knock."

Anthony Bloom (1, 62)

Today more than ever we need to recognize that the gift of solitude is not ordered to the acquisition of strange contemplative powers, but first of all to the recovery of one's deep self, and to the renewal of an authenticity which is twisted out of shape by the pretentious routines of a disordered togetherness. . . . [We must] be first of all a *person* who can give himself because he has a self to give. And indeed, we cannot give Christ if we have not found him, and we cannot find him if we cannot find ourselves.

Thomas Merton (4, 280–81)

Solitude. Where does its value lie? For in solitude we are in the presence of mere matter (even the sky, the stars, the moon, trees in blossom), things of less value (perhaps) than a human spirit. [Solitude's] value lies in the greater possibility of attention. If we could be attentive to the same degree in the presence of a human being. . . .

Simone Weil (2, 110)

We need to find God, and he cannot be found in noise and restlessness. God is the friend of silence. See how nature—trees, flowers, grass— grows in silence; see the stars, the moon, and the sun, how they move in silence. Is not our mission to give God to the poor in the slums? Not a dead God, but a living, loving God. The more we receive in silent prayer, the more we can give in our active life. We need silence to be able to touch souls. The essential thing is not what we say, but what God says to us and through us. All our words will be useless unless they come from within; words that do not give the light of Christ increase the darkness.

Mother Teresa of Calcutta (2, 68–69)

Have you ever been "stricken with silence?" If so, you have tasted the in-effable; you have had a mystical experience. Silence is too often defined as "the absence of something" when it is much more than that. Silence is also a search for something, a search for the depths, for the source.

Matthew Fox (2, 59)

[This is part of Rahner's "recipe" for how to "celebrate Christmas":] Have the courage to be alone. Only once you have really managed to do this, and have achieved it in a Christian way, can you hope to give the present of a heart filled with the Christmas spirit—in other words, a gentle, patient, courageously collected, softly tender heart—to those whom you are striving to love. *This* present is indeed something you should place under the Christmas tree, otherwise all other presents will simply be an unnecessary expense which could be incurred at any time of the year. And so for once try to endure your own company for a while. Perhaps you can find a room where you can be alone. Or you may know a lonely walk or a quiet church. . . . So: stop, be silent, wait. . . . You must allow yourself to approach silently nearer and nearer to yourself . . . all the waters of your life which flow away and run out and which are collected in the one basin of a heart aware of itself. Perhaps you will then begin to feel quite horrified by what you see. Perhaps the bitter waters of disgust, of hollowness, emptiness and boredom will rise out of the depths to the surface of your heart. . . . Endure yourself! . . . [In this stillness, emptiness, you will encounter] a mute pointer in the direction of God, something which in its namelessness and boundlessness gives us a hint that God is more than just another thing, added to those with which we normally have to deal. It points to *Him*. Through it, He allows us to become aware of his presence, if we are quiet and do not take fright and run away from the mysterious being which lives and acts in this silence.

Karl Rahner (2, 24–27)

True silence is a suspension bridge that a soul in love with God builds to cross the dark, frightening gullies of its own mind, the strange chasms of temptation, the depthless precipices of its own fears that impede its way to God.

True silence is the speech of lovers. For only love knows its beauty, completeness, and utter joy. True silence is a garden enclosed, where alone the soul can meet its God. It is a sealed fountain that he alone can unseal to slacken the soul's infinite thirst for him.

True silence is a key to the immense and flaming heart of God. It is the beginning of a divine courtship that will end only in the immense, creative, fruitful, loving silence of final union with the Beloved.

Catherine de Hueck Doherty (20–21)

One of the first steps toward solitude is a departure. Were you to depart to a real desert, you might take a plane, train or car to get there. But we're blind to the "little departures" that fill our days. These "little solitudes" are often right behind a door which we can open, or in a little corner where we can stop to look at a tree that somehow survived the snow and dust of a city street.

Catherine de Hueck Doherty (22)

Deserts, silence, solitude. For a soul that realizes the tremendous need of all three, opportunities present themselves in the midst of the congested trappings of all the world's immense cities.

Catherine de Hueck Doherty (23)

When you are able to create a lonely place in the middle of your actions and concerns, your successes and failures slowly can lose some of their power over you. For then your love for this world can merge with a compassionate understanding of its illusions. Then your serious engagement can merge with an unmasking smile. Then your concern for others can be motivated more by their needs than your own. In short: then you can care. Let us therefore live our lives to the fullest but let us not forget to once in a while get up long before dawn to leave the house and go to a lonely place.

Henri Nouwen (7, 26)

As long as we are occupied and preoccupied with our desire to do good but are not able to feel the crying need of those who suffer, our help remains hanging somewhere between our minds and our hands and does not descend into the heart where we can care. But in solitude, our heart can slowly take off its many protective devices, and can grow so wide and deep that nothing human is strange to it.

Henri Nouwen (7, 45)

Solitude is . . . the place of purification and transformation, the place of the great struggle and the great encounter. Solitude is not simply a means to an end. Solitude is its own end. It is the place where Christ re-models us in his own image and frees us from the victimizing compulsions of the world. Solitude is the place of our salvation.

Henri Nouwen (11, 18)

If I cannot receive the gifts of the Spirit in silence, I will never be able to receive them in any other way.

Madeleine L'Engle (3, 152)

Parallel Scripture Passages

Psalm 37:3–7   1 Kings 19:1–18
Psalm 46:10   Zechariah 2:13
Matthew 4:1–11   Psalm 62:5–8
Luke 6:12

GLEANINGS

Spiritual Presence and Incarnation

Thanks to the multitude of individuals and vocations, the Spirit of God insinuates itself everywhere and is everywhere at work. It is the great tree . . . whose sunlit branches refine and turn to flowers the sap extracted by the humblest of its roots.

Pierre Teilhard de Chardin (1, 109)

We cannot take one step towards the heavens. God crosses the universe and comes to us.

Simone Weil (5, 181)

God needs nothing of our wealth. But he does need our poverty, through which, alone, we may receive his gifts, his love, himself. God is not able to be himself, to be love, if he is not able to be self-outpouring into our hearts in the extravagant folly of his gratuitous love.

A Carthusian (28)

The heart of Christianity is the self-emptying, kenotic humility of God expressed in Jesus the Christ. . . .

At the heart of God's humility is this: God willingly is wounded.

Maggie Ross (3, xvi)

The humility of Christ: we seem to have forgotten that for any worship, thought, or activity to be called "Christian" it must be rooted in the humility of Christ.

Maggie Ross (3, xvii)

Because spiritual love does not desire but rather serves, it loves an enemy as a brother. It originates neither in the brother nor in the enemy but in Christ and his Word. Human love can never understand spiritual love, for spiritual love is from above; it is something completely strange, new, and incomprehensible to all earthly love.

Dietrich Bonhoeffer (4, 35)

There are three starting points of contemplation about God; three trails that lead to Him. The first is the way of sensing the presence of God in the world, in things; the second is the way of sensing His presence in the Bible; the third is the way of sensing His presence in sacred deeds. These three ways are intimated in three Biblical passages:

Lift up your eyes on high and see, Who created these?
Isaiah 40:26

I am the Lord thy God.
Exodus 20:2

We shall do and we shall hear.
Exodus 24:7

Abraham Heschel (31)

The entire meaning of Christian faith, and its uniqueness relative to all other religions, is that when it looks at the man Jesus it sees *God revealed*, God appearing in our midst, on earth, in time, in all the concreteness of the visible, perceptible, tangible world.

Alexander Schmemann (1, 47)

The Incarnation is the ultimate reason why the service of God cannot be divorced from the service of man. He who says he loves God and hates his brother is a liar.

There is therefore only one way of following Jesus and of worshiping God, and that is to be reconciled with our brethren.

Dietrich Bonhoeffer (1, 117)

Christ's presence can only be due to the operation of charity. It is obvious that Christ is in the man whose charity is perfectly pure; for who could be Christ's benefactor except Christ himself? And it is easy to understand that only Christ's presence in a soul can put true compassion in it. But the Gospel reveals further that he who gives from true compassion gives Christ himself.

Simone Weil (5, 191)

Slowly a light is beginning to dawn. I'm beginning to understand something I have known for a long time: You are still in the process of Your coming. Your appearance in the form of a slave was only the beginning of Your coming, a beginning in which You chose to redeem men by embracing the very slavery from which You were freeing them. And *You* can really achieve Your purpose in this paradoxical way, because the paths that *You* tread have a real ending, the narrow passes which *You* enter soon open out into broad liberty, the cross that *You* carry inevitably becomes a brilliant banner of triumph.

Karl Rahner (1, 85)

The Word of God has a cosmological border. It illuminates the world. It makes it known—heaven and Earth—as the sphere in which God's glory dwells and in which He concerns Himself with man.

Karl Barth (2, 11)

Jesus Christ is God's work and word. He is the fire of God's love, by which all theological existence is consumed even more radically than all human existence.

Karl Barth (4, 153)

God reveals himself everywhere, beneath our groping efforts, *as a universal milieu,* only because he is *the ultimate point* upon which all realities converge.

Pierre Teilhard de Chardin (1, 114)

In the divine *milieu* all the elements of the universe *touch each other* by that which is most inward and ultimate in them.

Pierre Teilhard de Chardin (1, 114)

The immense enchantment of the divine *milieu* owes all its value in the long run to the human-divine contact which was revealed at the Epiphany of Jesus.

Pierre Teilhard de Chardin (1, 117)

Christ—for whom and in whom we are formed, each with his own individuality and his own vocation—Christ reveals himself in each reality around us, and shines like an ultimate determinant, like a centre, one might almost say like a universal element.

Pierre Teilhard de Chardin (1, 125)

God is no White Knight who charges into the world to pluck us like distressed damsels from the jaws of dragons, or diseases. God chooses to become present to and through us. It is up to us to rescue one another.

Nancy Mairs (179)

"Ubi caritas, Deus ibi est." Where charity and love are, God is there.

Nancy Mairs (180)

Halakhic man . . . longs to bring transcendence down into this valley of the shadow of death—i.e., into our world—and transform it into a land of the living. *Homo religiosus* [religious man] is a romantic who chafes against concrete reality and tries to flee to distant worlds that will restore his spirits and their purity and pristine clarity. Halakhic man, however, takes up his position in this world and does not move from it. He wishes to purify this world, not to escape from it. . . . His goal is not flight to another world that is wholly good, but rather bringing down the eternal world into the midst of our world. . . . Halakhic man craves to bring down the divine presence and holiness into the midst of space and time, into the midst of finite, earthly existence.

Joseph Soloveitchik (2, 40–41)

An individual does not become holy through mystical adhesion to the absolute nor through mysterious union with the infinite, nor through a boundless, all-embracing ecstasy, but, rather, through his whole biological life, through his animal actions, and through actualizing the Halakhah in the empirical world.

Joseph Soloveitchik (2, 46)

The task of man is to bring down the Divine Presence to the lower world, to this vale of tears. The mystery of *Tzimtzum*[4] should not precipitate metaphysical anguish but rather gladness and joy. Man resides together with his Creator in this world, and it is only through cultivating that togetherness in the here and now that man can acquire a share in the world to come.

Joseph Soloveitchik (2, 52)

The fact that Christ *comes* and is *present* was far more significant than the places where He had been.

Alexander Schmemann (2, 20)

In my tradition, an immunity system exists from the beginning. God is irremediably on the side of life, creates life from inert dust, cherishes life, finally sends an embassy of life, a very Son. A true blood brother. His ethic is one with his life and death, his initiatives and commands issue from the deepest springs of grace; love your enemies, do good to those who lay violent hands on you. Thus you become godlike.

Daniel Berrigan (4, 21)

[Mary] is the *Mother of Christ.* She is the fullness of love accepting the coming of God to us—giving life to Him, who is the Life of the world. And the whole creation rejoices in her, because it recognizes through her that the end and fulfillment of all life, of all love *is to accept Christ,* to give Him life in ourselves.

Alexander Schmemann (2, 87)

It is *this world* (and not any "other world"), it is *this life* (and not some "other life") that were given to man to be a sacrament of the divine presence, given as communion with God, and it is only through this world, this life, by "transforming" them into communion with God that man *was to be.* . . . It is when Life weeps at the grave of the friend, when it contemplates the horror of death, that the victory over death begins.

Alexander Schmemann (2, 100)

When Gagarin[5] came back from space and made his remarkable statement that he never saw God in Heaven, one of our priests in Moscow remarked, "If you have not seen Him on Earth, you will never see Him in Heaven."

Anthony Bloom (1, 45)

Every step I had taken, from the Absolute to "Spirit" and from "Spirit" to "God," had been a step toward the more concrete, the more imminent, the more compulsive. At each step one had less chance "to call one's soul one's own." To accept the Incarnation was a further step in the same direction. It brings God nearer, or near in a new way. And this, I found, was something I had not wanted. But to recognize the ground for my evasion was of course to recognize both its shame and its futility.

C. S. Lewis (4, 237)

Images of the Holy easily become holy images—sacrosanct. My idea of God is not a divine idea. It has to be shattered time after time. He shatters it Himself. He is the great iconoclast. . . . The Incarnation is the supreme example; it leaves all previous ideas of the Messiah in ruins.

C. S. Lewis (1, 76)

Has it never happened to you to lose yourself for a moment in a swift and satisfying experience for which you found no name? When the world took on a strangeness, and you rushed out to meet it, in a mood at once exultant and ashamed? Was there not an instant when you took the lady who now orders your dinner into your arms, and she suddenly interpreted to you the whole of the universe? A universe so great, charged with so terrible an intensity, that you have hardly dared to think of it since. Do you remember that horrid moment at the concert, when you became wholly unaware of your comfortable seven-and-sixpenny seat? Those were onsets of involuntary contemplation; sudden partings of the conceptual veil. Dare you call them the least significant moments of your life?

Evelyn Underhill (2, 30)

Parallel Scripture Passages

1 Corinthians 3:16	Galatians 2:19–21	Acts 2:14–21
John 1:1–5	Philippians 2:1–13	Ezekiel 37:1–14
Philippians 1:6	1 Corinthians 6:16–17	Romans 8:9–13
Galatians 3:25–29	Joel 3:1–2	1 John 3:14–20
Ephesians 4:11–16	John 3:3–8	

GLEANINGS

Struggle and Wholeness

To live the tension of the world is the highest test of our being.

Martin Buber (2, 143)

From **Prayer for the Rich**

Help all those
who have made themselves rich,
even if perhaps through hard work:
convince them
that the best inheritance they can leave their children
is the living example
of justice,
of the open heart and the open hand,
of freedom from money
by using it for service
and not making an idol of it.

Dom Helder Camara (1, 73)

Christian ethics is in no sense dualistic. It allows no split or separation, no glance into a present without a beyond, and no glance into a beyond without seeing its light shining into the present. It allows no talk of prayer which does not of itself lead into work, and no talk of work which is not grounded in prayer. It knows no soul apart from body, nor a body apart from soul, no private sphere without public responsibility, and no public responsibility without the quiet pose of privacy. Christian ethics has to do with man, who is wholly lost, wholly rescued and therefore is claimed as a whole man.

Karl Barth (6, 93)

Do not wait for leaders; do it alone, person to person.

Mother Teresa of Calcutta (2, 34)

Without integrity, relationships that call themselves sacred become demonic.

Maggie Ross (4, 61)

Fr. [Jean] de Menasce told somebody not to come into the Church until he felt it would be an enlargement of his freedom. . . . I suppose it is like marriage, that when you get into it, you find it is the beginning, not the end, of the struggle to make love work.

Flannery O'Connor (1, 93)

This kind of split makes me crazy, this territorializing of the holy. Here God may dwell, Here God may not dwell. It contradicts everything in my experience, which says: God dwells where I dwell. Period.

Nancy Mairs (10)

The point is not esoteric but of immediate practical consequence: whatever else may be affirmed about a spirituality which has biblical precedent and style, spiritual maturity or spiritual fulfillment necessarily involves the *whole* person—body, mind, soul, place, relationships—in connection with the whole of creation throughout the era of time. Biblical spirituality encompasses the whole person in the totality of existence in this world, not some fragment or scrap or incident of a person. This book has no other aim than to commend, thus, the efficacy of the Incarnation.

William Stringfellow (3, 22)

If you want to escape from Hindrance, do not try to augment your power in proportion to the covetousness of pride and ambition, for Hindrance will augment in like measure. Reduce your desires to your needs, your ambition to surpassing yourself and your pride to considering the dignity of your essence.

Lanza del Vasto (2, 89)

The extreme greatness of Christianity lies in the fact that it does not seek a supernatural remedy for suffering but a supernatural use for it.

Simone Weil (2, 73)

I would rather suffer all the pain in the world than reach the sort of wisdom that would make everything appear indifferent and vain.

Christ, deliver me always from indifference and make known to me the fullness of things.

Lanza del Vasto (2, 102)

What do you do with your life when your life is irretrievably stuck?

Answer: Your choices are narrow, but there are still choices. You either (1) stop living, thus adding another corpse to the ethical ossuary, or (2) you get unstuck, you walk out on the death scene, responsibly.

Daniel Berrigan (2, 69)

[Gandhi asked Lanza del Vasto a series of questions about his vocation:]

"Are you called? Or is it you who are calling yourself? Or are you forcing yourself to believe yourself called? . . .

"Ask yourself, 'Is it God's Will or mine?' That is the only important question."

Lanza del Vasto (3, 259–60)

True peace *is* engagement with darkness, a steady course that travels through its heart, through the flames of purification. When I was willing to stop trying to conform to a limited model, when I ceased trying to manipulate grace at work in the depths of my being, only then, by allowing this process to run its natural course, could I begin to understand the nature of true peace. . . .

I began to understand the wise monk's simple word: "In the struggle to forgive you are forgiving, and healing the others, too, even though there may be no awareness."

Maggie Ross (4, 106)

What is essential for each one of us is to know our needs (they vary from person to person) and to find a way to realize them, or a path of purification that is consonant with the values and state of life that we have chosen. The formula will be different for each one and will be subject to revision throughout life. What must be avoided is an existence in which unrecognized needs are repressed and look for satisfaction in various guises, contrary to the gospel values to which we want to commit ourselves. One of the reasons it is so difficult to find and maintain a healthy equilibrium in our life is the limited range of possibilities that it offers for the realization of human needs. The solitary life necessarily places itself under the sign of the Cross, of a radical transfiguration that cannot be fruitful except under the influence of great love. We must begin with an intense spiritual life and an adequately developed human maturity. We can't take short cuts with impunity. We can renounce only what we possess, one way or another.

A Carthusian, 17th Conference, July 1978[1]

[After a distasteful encounter regarding the sanctity of our bodies with a Catholic chaplain at the University of Arizona named Brother Tim, Nancy Mairs wrote:]

I wanted to put my arms protectively around anyone Brother Tim had spoken to and whisper: *The world may well end if you cut down its trees and pave it over; it may well end if you permit its people to go unfed and unclothed and uneducated while you prosper. But the world will not end if you touch your genitals. The world will not end even if you touch someone else's genitals. I can think of sound reasons for choosing not to do so, but fear and disgust should not be among them. Your body is not a pesthouse, it is simply a body: who you are: part of God's creation, a small part, true, but as real and lovely as the rest. If you love every part, evil will not enter the world through you. Through Brother Tim, maybe, but not through you.*

Nancy Mairs (203)

I know now the only way to cope with growing up is to become like a little child: to evolve with all our complexity to simplicity; to accept and to trust as a little child trusts, only now with the reconstituted innocence born of sin and pain redeemed that is more precious than the first innocence, and which enables us to walk into the dark closet knowing we will be clobbered, but walking in, trusting, anyway. To love wholeheartedly with wonder and astonishment and delight; to not be afraid of the self-forgetful child's absorption in life, approached uncritically and with suspended judgment.

Maggie Ross (1, 130)

God created and it was joy: time, space, matter. There *is,* and we are part of that is-ness, part of that becoming. That is our calling: co-creation. Every single one of us, without exception, is called to co-create with God. No one is too unimportant to have a share in the making or unmaking of the final showing-forth. Everything that we do either draws the Kingdom of love closer, or pushes it further off.

Madeleine L'Engle (1, 19)

The problem of pain, of war and the horror of war, of poverty and disease is always confronting us. But a God who allows no pain, no grief, also allows no choice. There is little unfairness in a colony of ants, but also there is little freedom. We human beings have been given the terrible gift of free will, and this ability to make choices, to help write our own story, is what makes us human, even when we make the wrong choices, abusing our freedom and the freedom of others.

Madeleine L'Engle (6, 25–26)

What can we gain by sailing to the moon if we are not able to cross the abyss that separates us from ourselves? This is the most important of all voyages of discovery, and without it all the rest are not only useless but disastrous.

Thomas Merton (8, 11)

And that is why we experience Joy: we yearn, rightly, for that unity which we can never reach except by ceasing to be the separate phenomenal beings called "we." Joy was not a deception. Its visitations were rather the moments of clearest consciousness we had, when we became aware of our fragmentary and phantasmal nature and ached for that impossible reunion which would annihilate us or that self-contradictory waking which would reveal, not that we had had, but that we *were*, a dream.

C. S. Lewis (4, 221–22)

Good and evil both increase at compound interest. That is why the little decisions you and I make every day are of such infinite importance. The smallest good act today is the capture of a strategic point from which, a few months later, you may be able to go on to victories you never dreamed of.

C. S. Lewis (2, 117)

The road is long and hard and difficult. Never be afraid. You won't be if you understand where you are and why you are there. You won't be afraid—but you might be awed. Somewhere along the road you will meet evil. For whenever God reveals himself, he must allow you to meet the other one, who is also a part of his creation. It is not that you are grasping at the forbidden fruit of the tree, but God allows a confrontation with it. You have to know how to encounter evil at God's bidding, at his time, in order to be able to contribute to the community of man. For evil is among us.

Catherine de Hueck Doherty (114)

If the world despises one of the brethren, the Christian will love and serve him. If the world does him violence, the Christian will succour and comfort him. If the world dishonours and insults him, the Christian will sacrifice his own honour to cover his brother's shame. Where the world seeks gain, the Christian will renounce it. Where the world exploits, he will dispossess himself, and where the world oppresses, he will stoop down and raise up the oppressed.

Dietrich Bonhoeffer (1, 232)

Sometimes the hurly-burly of our emotional life, which threatens to overwhelm us, is mysteriously stilled. Sometimes events, which we think must destroy us or those whom we love, are strangely modified by the Spirit that indwells and rules them. More and more as we go on with the Christian life we learn the absolute power of Spirit over circumstance.

Evelyn Underhill (1, 70)

God too has a geography. He stands somewhere. Where that is, the psalm [Psalm 94] gives more than a hint. In this poem and others, it is clear that He stands, and stands and stands, in one and the same place: at the side of the just, in the midst of trouble, facing the adversaries. And that would seem to be the point of this prayer, and of any prayer for help in distress. Not that God must be drawn by threads or cables out of His empyrean neutrality; but that He is near, at hand, at all times, but most pressingly (one almost said breathingly) when justice is assailed, and the life or death of the innocent is in question.

Daniel Berrigan (3, 94–95)

Parallel Scripture Passages

Psalm 27:11–14	2 Timothy 2:1–9	1 Peter 5:6–11
Psalm 138	Psalm 30	1 Corinthians 2:1–5
Isaiah 40:28–31	2 Corinthians 1:3–7	2 Corinthians 12:1–10
2 Corinthians 4:16–18	Isaiah 25:4–9	

GLEANINGS

Suffering and Compassion

We must make our homes centers of compassion and forgive endlessly.
Mother Teresa of Calcutta (2, 12)

God's goodness is not a cosmic force but a specific act of compassion.
Abraham Heschel (21)

Praise to God and Compassion for creatures.
It is the same movement of the heart.
Simone Weil (1, 102)

The near God is the God of the heart, the heart which is never as much itself, and nothing but itself, as when it suffers.
Franz Rosenzweig (281)

For our God makes only one demand upon us. He does not expect a humanly unattainable completeness and perfection, but only the willingness to do as much as we possibly can at every single instant.
Martin Buber (4, 320)

Suffering is increasing in the world today. People are hungry for something more beautiful, for something greater than people round about can give. There is a great hunger for God in the world today. Everywhere there is much suffering, but there is also great hunger for God and love for each other.

Mother Teresa of Calcutta (2, 19)

Whether we knew and valued them [the victims of the Second World War and National Socialism] or not, they were our neighbors, our human brothers and sisters. . . . They fell in a cause for which we are partly responsible. And they ask us, these victims of war, for what really did they fall and die and drown, for what did they suffer among us, sick and crippled. . . . It would be totally unworthy if we were to forget them and repulse their questions. It would also be impossible; we cannot escape them.

Karl Barth (7, 77–78)

It is not some religious act which makes a Christian what he is, but participation in the suffering of God in the life of the world.

Dietrich Bonhoeffer (3, 223)

You will have found Christ when you are concerned with other people's sufferings and not your own.

Flannery O'Connor (1, 453)

In true love it is not we who love the afflicted in God; it is God in us who loves them. When we are in affliction, it is God in us who loves those who wish us well. Compassion and gratitude come down from God, and when they are exchanged in a glance, God is present at the point where the eyes of those who give and those who receive meet.

Simone Weil (7, 151)

Poor and afflicted and oppressed people have faces, and we are required to look squarely into them. We can't love what we won't experience.

Nancy Mairs (168)

Being poor is also a way of feeling, knowing, reasoning, making friends, loving, believing, suffering, celebrating, and praying. The poor constitute a world of their own. Commitment to the poor means entering, and in some cases remaining in, that universe with a much clearer awareness; it means being one of its inhabitants, looking upon it as a place of residence and not simply of work. It does not mean going into that world by the hour to bear witness to the gospel, but rather emerging from within it each morning in order to proclaim the good news to every human being.

Gustavo Gutiérrez (2, 125)

Here is the true meaning and value of compassion and non-violence when it helps us to see the enemy's point of view, to hear his questions, to know his assessment of ourselves. For from his view we may indeed see the basic weaknesses of our own condition, and if we are mature we may learn and grow and profit from the wisdom of the brothers who are called the opposition.

Martin Luther King Jr. (1, 5)

Compassion consists in paying attention to an afflicted man and identifying oneself with him in thought. It then follows that one feeds him automatically if he is hungry, just as one feeds oneself. Bread given in this way is the effect and the sign of compassion. This is what Christ thanks us for.

Simone Weil (1, 327)

Sometime in your life, hope that you might see one starved man, the look on his face when the bread finally arrives. Hope that you might have baked it or bought it or even kneaded it yourself. For that look on his face for your meeting his eyes across a piece of bread, you might be willing to lose a lot, or suffer a lot, or die a little even.

Daniel Berrigan, from an address given
at The College of Wooster, February 1991

God is absent from the world, except in the existence in this world of those in whom His love is alive. Therefore they ought to be present to the world through compassion. Their compassion is the visible presence of God here below.

When we are lacking in compassion we make a violent separation between a creature and God. . . .

Compassion . . . is the rainbow.

Simone Weil (1, 103)

As tears are intimately related to, even synonymous with *kenosis, we find at the bottom of our tears that it is God who weeps and God who weeps with us.* Here is the exchange of love; here is the gathering of all our pain and all our joy.

These are the tears that wash Ezekiel the prophet; these are the tears of living water from the well of Jacob; these tears are the living water from the side of Christ, from the wound that incorporates all our wounds, and in which our lives are hidden and from which our new life comes.

It is God's tears we weep as God seeks humbly to become incarnate in us through the meeting and mingling of God's tears and ours.

And from this mingling of tears the will of God is born.

Maggie Ross (2, 204)

There are also tears that are not bitter. They are like the dew of the morning, gentle, silent, springing from the depths of the heart, we know not why. They do not have a name; they have no cause. Sometimes these are tears of joy, a quiet joy, from the depths, far deeper than our superficial feelings, tears born from the silence of solitude when suddenly the life of stillness takes on a luminous intensity—or rather, we become aware of the intense reality of the life in which we are immersed. Why weep? I do not know. Perhaps it is because of the utter gratuitousness of life, of being, which we experience in such moments, like the occasions when we know what it is to be loved, truly, deeply, for ourselves. Such a gift is so beautiful, so grand! They are tears of gratitude, of wonder, of love. These tears can be entirely interior, as they arise from the ground of the hidden heart, or they may be exterior as well. It very much depends on temperament and cultural conditioning.

A Carthusian (30)

"Not enough world for need and greed." An old saying of Peter Maurin newly verified, as indeed the world proves not big enough, not rich enough, to bear the burden of bodily hunger and cupidity of spirit.

We had always thought there was enough: water enough, air and land enough, minerals enough, food enough, America enough, world enough.

Or at least those in possession thought so; for the others, of course, the question did not really signify anything. The earth was ours; for them, was not heaven enough?

Daniel Berrigan (3, 55–56)

The charity that begins at home cannot rest there but draws one inexorably over the threshold and off the porch and down the street and so out and out and out and out into the world which becomes the home wherein charity begins until it becomes possible, in theory at least, to love the whole of creation with the same patience, affection, and amusement one first practiced, in between the pouts and tantrums, with parents, siblings, spouse, and children.

Nancy Mairs (176)

God enters the world through those of us who are willing to let God participate fully in our lives, in our sufferings as well as our celebrations. Through suffering with us, God empowers us to carry out the will of God: that we assume full responsibility not only for our own suffering but for the suffering of others. We are not pitiful creatures huddled helplessly beneath a blizzard of miseries blown down by some capricious power amusing himself at our expense. God is with(in) each of us, and to the extent that we recognize and honor God's presence in one another, we form and dwell in the Community of God.

Nancy Mairs (185–86)

We are not permitted to choose the frame of our destiny. But what we put into it is ours. He who wills adventure will experience it—according to the measure of his courage. He who wills sacrifice will be sacrificed—according to the measure of his purity of heart.

Dag Hammarskjöld (55)

It is infinitely easier to suffer in obedience to a human command than to accept suffering as free, responsible men. It is infinitely easier to suffer with others than to suffer alone. It is infinitely easier to suffer as public heroes than to suffer apart and in ignominy. It is infinitely easier to suffer physical death than to endure spiritual suffering. Christ suffered as a free man alone, apart and in ignominy, in body and in spirit, and since that day many Christians have suffered with him.

Dietrich Bonhoeffer (3, 31)

The horror of evil is that it has turned suffering into something normal, and that together with death, it has become the only absolute law of the world and of life.

Alexander Schmemann (1, 84)

Suffering as disintegration of life is transformed by Christ into the possibility of being born to genuine spiritual life.

Alexander Schmemann (1, 85)

The heavenly banquet cannot begin until we are all there, and I can greet with love . . . everybody who has caused me pain, and call out a welcome to them all. The heavenly banquet cannot begin until all those whom I have hurt are ready to welcome me, in all my flawed and contradictory humanness.

Forgiveness which leads to welcoming, with open arms, the forgiven ones to the party, comes less from an act of will than from a gift of grace. Sometimes prayer opens the door to this gift.

Madeleine L'Engle (5, 51)

When we are in communion with the Creator we are less afraid, less afraid that the wrong people will come to the party, less afraid that we ourselves aren't good enough, less afraid of pain and alienation and death. . . . Because Jesus cried out in anguish, we may, too. But our fear is less frequent and infinitely less if we are close to the Creator. Jesus, having cried out, then let his fear go, and moved on.

Madeleine L'Engle (4, 211)

In truth, compassion is the very origin and goal—as well as the process—of creation mysticism. "The first outburst of everything God does," Meister Eckhart says, "is compassion." This means that all creatures as children of God hold compassion in common. Compassion is our universal heritage, our God-origin and our God-destiny. Compassion unites us, it forms the common "field" that all creatures share. The mystic intuits this, feels it, experiences it, tries to live it out in some fashion.

Matthew Fox (2, 50)

To experience compassion and to identify with the suffering of others—as well as with their joy—is to experience the Divine One who suffers and rejoices in each person. To struggle to birth one's own "I am" is also to experience the divine "I am." In fact, we must all birth the Cosmic Christ in our being and doing for that is why we exist. Is not the purpose of the incarnation in Jesus to reveal the imminence of the Cosmic Christ in the sufferings and dignity of each creature of the Earth? As we discover our own "I am" and the ecstasy and pain of the Divine One in us, we gradually grow into an "I-am-with" others (*Emmanuel*, "God-with-us"). We grow in compassion and in doing so the divine "I am" takes on flesh once again. Since God alone is the Compassionate One, as we grow into compassion we also grow into our divinity.

Matthew Fox (2, 155)

Now error and sin both have this property, that the deeper they are the less their victim suspects their existence; they are masked evil. Pain is unmasked, unmistakable evil; every man knows that something is wrong when he is being hurt.

C. S. Lewis (3, 92)

What is good in any painful experience is, for the sufferer, his submission to the will of God, and, for the spectators, the compassion aroused and the acts of mercy to which it leads.

C. S. Lewis (3, 110)

Suffering makes one more sensitive to the pain in the world. It can teach us to put forth a greater love for everything that exists.

Dorothee Soelle (1, 125)

To attain the image of Christ means to live in revolt against the great Pharaoh and to remain with the oppressed and the disadvantaged. It means to make their lot one's own. It is easy to be on Pharaoh's side if one just blinks an eye. It is easy to overlook the crosses by which we are surrounded.

Dorothee Soelle (1, 132)

Compassion lies at the heart of our prayer for our fellow human beings. When I pray for the world, I become the world: when I pray for the endless needs of the millions, my soul expands and wants to embrace them all and bring them into the presence of God. But in the midst of that experience, I realize that compassion is not mine but God's gift to me. I cannot embrace the world, but God can. I cannot pray, but God can pray in me. When God became as we are, that is when God allowed all of us to enter into his intimate life, it became possible for us to share in his infinite compassion.

Henri Nouwen (1, 123)

True compassion is more than flinging a coin to a beggar; it is not haphazard and superficial. It comes to see that an edifice which produces beggars needs re-structuring.

Martin Luther King Jr. (1, 8–9)

Real care is not ambiguous. Real care excludes indifference and is the opposite of apathy. The word "care" finds its roots in the Gothic "Kara" which means lament. The basic meaning of care is: to grieve, to experience sorrow, to cry out with. I am very much struck by this background of the word care because we tend to look at caring as an attitude of the strong toward the weak, of the powerful toward the powerless, of the have's toward the have-not's. And, in fact, we feel quite uncomfortable with an invitation to enter into someone's pain before doing something about it.

Henri Nouwen (7, 33–34)

Compassion also means sharing another's joy which can be just as difficult as suffering with him. To give another the chance to be completely happy and to let his joy blossom to the full.

Henri Nouwen (12, 112)

Our sufferings and pains are not simply bothersome interruptions of our lives; rather, they touch us in our uniqueness and our most intimate individuality. The way I am broken tells you something unique about me. The way you are broken tells me something unique about you. That is the reason for my feeling very privileged when you freely share some of your deep pain with me, and that is why it is an expression of my trust in you when I disclose to you something of my vulnerable side.

Henri Nouwen (4, 71)

Compassion is hard because it requires the inner disposition to go with others to the place where they are weak, vulnerable, lonely, and broken.

But this is not our spontaneous response to suffering. What we desire most is to do away with suffering by fleeing from it or finding a quick cure for it. As busy, active, relevant ministers, we want to earn our bread by making a real contribution. This means first and foremost doing something to show that our presence makes a difference. And so we ignore our greatest gift, which is our ability to enter into solidarity with those who suffer.

Henri Nouwen (11, 20)

Parallel Scripture Passages

Luke 6:32–38   Revelation 7:13–17
Colossians 3:12–15   Hebrews 2:5–18
Deuteronomy 10:14–21   Isaiah 40:1–11
Psalm 41:1–3   Mark 1:39–41
Mark 12:41–44

GLEANINGS

Worship,
Gratitude, and Joy

In a sacred deed, we echo God's suppressed chant; in loving we intone God's unfinished song.

Abraham Heschel (290)

Of all accusations against Christians, the most terrible one was uttered by Nietzsche when he said that Christians had no joy.

Alexander Schmemann (2, 24)

It is man's duty to fulfil his task by pure means and to hope in God. The ploughman turns the earth over and sows seed in it. He does not make the wheat grow. The crop is therefore not due to him. So when he has sown, he must pray, and if he reaps he must give thanks.

Lanza del Vasto (3, 144)

To think of God man must hear the world. Man is not alone in celebrating God. To praise Him is to join all things in their song to Him. Our kinship with nature is a kinship of praise. All beings praise God. We live in a community of praise.

Abraham Heschel (95)

If God were a theory, the study of theology would be the way to understand Him. But God is alive and in need of love and worship.

Abraham Heschel (281)

Torah without a tune is devoid of spirit. Kavanah is the art of setting a deed to inner music. "Come before His presence with singing" (Psalm 100:2). In singing we enter His presence.

Abraham Heschel (355)

[Writing to Eugen Rosenstock on why his Judaism was an inward affair, Rosenzweig says:] I would have to show you Judaism from within, that is, in a hymn.

Franz Rosenzweig (xxii)

"Sing and make melody in your heart to the Lord" (Eph. 5:19). . . . Where the heart is not singing there is no melody, there is only the dreadful medley of human self-praise. Where the singing is not to the Lord, it is singing to the honor of the self or the music, and the new song becomes a song to idols.

Dietrich Bonhoeffer (4, 58–59)

Worship and living are not two separate realms. Unless living is a form of worship, our worship has no life.

Abraham Heschel (384)

Worship is the celebration of life in its totality. Worship is the sacramental appropriation of all of life in celebration. Worship is the festival of creation.

William Stringfellow (4, 101)

Joy . . . is not something one can define or analyze. One enters into joy. "Enter thou into the joy of the Lord" (Matt. 25:21).

Alexander Schmemann (2, 25)

A Christian is the one who, wherever he looks, finds Christ and rejoices in Him. And this joy *transforms* all his human plans and programs, decisions and actions, making all his mission the sacrament of the world's return to Him who is the life of the world.

Alexander Schmemann (2, 113)

Be a sign of joy and of brotherly love among men.

Open yourself to all that is human and you will see any vain desire to flee from the world vanish from your heart. Be present to the time in which you live; adapt yourself to the conditions of the moment.

Brother Roger (1, 19)

Perfect joy is in the laying aside of self in peaceful love; to burst forth, this joy needs all your being.

Brother Roger (1, 63)

Let us rise in the morning and offer ourselves to God. We have woken from a sleep which divides us from yesterday. Waking up offers us a new reality, a day which has never existed before, an unknown time and space stretching before us like a field of untrodden snow. Let us ask the Lord to bless this day and bless us in it.

Anthony Bloom (2, 42)

The first act of prayer is to choose such words of prayer as are completely true to what you are, words which you are not ashamed of, which express you adequately and are worthy of you—and then offer them to God with all the intelligence of which you are capable. You must also put all the heart you can into an act of worship, an act of recognition of God, an act of cherishing, which is the true meaning of charity.

Anthony Bloom (1, 23)

Whenever I felt the beauty of the world in song or story, in the material universe around me, or glimpsed it in human love, I wanted to cry out with joy. The Psalms were an outlet for this enthusiasm of joy or grief— and I suppose my writing was also an outlet. After all, one must communicate ideas. I always felt the common unity of our humanity; the longing of the human heart is for this communion. If only I could sing, I thought, I would shout before the Lord, and call upon the world to shout with me, "All ye works of the Lord, bless ye the Lord, praise Him and glorify Him forever."

Dorothy Day (29)

Joy and sorrow, life and death, always so closely together!

Dorothy Day (242)

Love of God is pure when joy and suffering inspire an *equal* degree of gratitude.

Simone Weil (2, 55)

Only he who gives thanks for little things receives the big things. We prevent God from giving us the great spiritual gifts He has in store for us, because we do not give thanks for daily gifts.

Dietrich Bonhoeffer (4, 29)

Gratitude is one of the most visible characteristics of the poor I have come to know. I am always surrounded by words of thanks: "thanks for your visit, your blessing, your sermon, your prayer, your gifts, your presence with us." Even the smallest and most necessary goods are a reason for gratitude. This all-pervading gratitude is the basis for celebration. Not only are the poor grateful for life, but they also celebrate life constantly. A visit, a reunion, a simple meeting are always like little celebrations. . . . All of life is a gift, a gift to be celebrated, a gift to be shared.

Henri Nouwen (2, 146–47)

Joy is a net of love by which we can capture souls. God loves the person who gives with joy. Whoever gives with joy gives more. The best way to show our gratitude to God and to people is to accept with joy. Joy can thrive in a heart burning with love.

We wait impatiently for the paradise where God is, but we have it in our power to be in paradise with Him, right now; being happy with Him means:

> To love as He loves.
> To help as He helps.
> To give as He gives.
> To serve as He serves.

Mother Teresa of Calcutta (1, 61–62)

Parallel Scripture Passages

Psalm 50:8–15	Psalm 147	Colossians 3:16–17
Psalm 100	Psalm 148	1 John 1:1–5
Psalm 104	Psalm 149	Luke 1:40–55
Psalm 145	Psalm 150	John 16:20–24
Psalm 146	Ephesians 5:15–20	Romans 14:17–19

Some Practical Uses of Gleanings for Spiritual Reading and Spiritual Formation

In this book we have traced the sources of an emerging spirituality for the twenty-first century. We have offered gleanings from writers in this century who view every aspect of life from a spiritual perspective. It has been our intention not only to provide seeds for future harvest but to help the reader move beyond reflection on others' words into a personal experience of the sacred. We have gathered these gleanings as potential entry points into a new or renewed experience of the sacred. Our deepest intent has been to open windows into the spacious realm of the spirit, where the yearning for God, for wholeness of life, for holiness of living, resides.

For the person seeking a deeper and deepening relationship with God, the move from theological reflection to spiritual experience may need some further explanation. What we are inviting the reader to try is a move from an engagement of the mind, which *thinks* about God, to an engagement of the heart, which *meets* the immediacy of holy mystery. In this encounter with the presence of God, we may then be shaped by God's Spirit, formed more faithfully in God's image, transformed more fully into the people of God in our everyday lives.

This is a moment in which we "gaze on God" or "rest in God," a moment of contemplation that, by its nature, changes who we are in the next moment. The Old Testament holds an understanding of the power of this encounter. The people of that time thought that they could not look on God's face and live. Indeed, we die to our old selves in the encounter and are resurrected in its power for reformation of our deepest selves.

Over the centuries, many prayer forms and spiritual practices have been developed to assist those committed to this communion with the Divine. Many of them have come from monks, mystics, or revered teachers who spent their entire lives seeking the fullest experience of divinity within their human experience. It would be easy to dismiss their wisdom by denying that such focused spiritual life is possible for ordinary people. Many of the writers from whom we have gleaned offer us a different view. Thomas Merton, Matthew Fox, Evelyn Underhill, and others affirm the potential in each of us for a mystical experience that supports a life of activism. Parker Palmer, in his book *The Active Life: A Spirituality of Work, Creativity, and Caring,* puts it this way: "Contemplation and action are not high skills or specialties for the virtuoso few. They are the warp and weft of human life, the interaction threads that form the fabric of who we are and who we are becoming."[1]

One of the mystics who pursued the life of the spirit in the fourteenth century was Meister Eckhart. He said, "God is at home. It is we who have gone out for a walk."[2] The spirituality that we have described is a spirituality of homecoming, of seeking our home in God. It is one of the paradoxes of prayer, for example, that as soon as we are aware that we have been absent from ourselves and God, or have "left home," we have already made the first step in the homeward direction. To become aware of our homesickness is already to have journeyed halfway home. Indeed, sometimes a simple look over our shoulders in the homeward direction is enough to take us there. We find ourselves embraced by holy presence and nurtured by divine love simply by remembering what we have left or lost. The gleanings we have offered may be a means of remembering. They may offer a homeward glance toward God.

We offer now, in this Appendix, several prayer forms and spiritual disciplines that may serve as maps for those who are "homeward bound." The gleanings may gift the reader with a glance of remembrance. These practical helps give the opportunity for a long, deep gaze into the holy mystery that surrounds us.

We encourage the reader to try all of these prayer forms and then to practice one for a significant period of time. As with learning to dance, to play an instrument, or to bake bread, practice is important. With practice, it is possible at some point to forget the form and simply to dance, simply to play, simply to knead, simply to pray.

One caution seems wise. It is good to remember that these prayer forms are merely maps, not the terrain of the spiritual life itself. They provide only hints as to how to get there. They may be seen as recommendations from those who have traveled these routes and found them to provide good passage. In outline, they are not the path with all its ups and downs, curves and straightaways, lush gardens and desert wildernesses. The prayer form is not the prayer. The prayer is finally that experience of intimacy in which one knows that all the apparent separations and boundaries of life are illusions, that at the core of human experience is the holy. It has been there all along, patiently waiting for us, willing for us to sink into its deep and abiding love.

The point in all the following forms of spiritual reading or recalling or attending to God is to help the scripture or sacred text to penetrate our human life, to allow a spiritual writing or "gleaning" to take hold in one's life. So, from our gleanings, choose a passage on a topic that fits a need and turn it over in one of the ways suggested below.

LECTIO DIVINA (SPIRITUAL READING)

One of the oldest of spiritual disciplines, the *lectio divina*, takes a passage of scripture or a spiritual writing and uses it as a focus for prayer. It begins with a settling time of silence. Then it moves to reading a short passage, seeking the experience of encounter with God and the revelation of God's holy truth. In meditation, one reflects on the text, noticing what particular words or phrases stand out and letting them speak to one's heart as well as one's head. This meditation becomes a kind of conversation, a dialogue with Christ or with God in which understanding may deepen. Finally, words and ideas fall again into an inner silence in which the reader and the Holy One simply sit together in communion. It has been said that this means of prayer is like developing a friendship, cultivating an attitude of openness, trust, and love.

For help with this prayer form, see *Too Deep for Words: Rediscovering the Lectio Divina* (1988), by Thelma Hall.

CENTERING PRAYER

In this prayer form, a word or short phrase becomes the focus for centering oneself in God's presence. It is like a bell that calls us to remember and draws our attention back to God.

In traditional centering prayer, one sits in silence, having cleared the mind of images and thoughts and having cleared the heart of distracting emotions. In the silence, one waits for a word or phrase to rise out of the depths of that silent openness. The word may be very simple: love, hope, peace, comfort, joy. It may also be a simple phrase, easy to remember, as long as it is "given" and not a manipulated choice one thinks about on one's own. After the gift of the word, one sits in silence, seeking to be aware of God, willing to receive God's grace, resting in God's love. When small or large distractions arise, something that comes into this still presence, then one speaks inwardly that word or phrase as a way of returning to God, of "centering" again in the open and spacious silence and presence of God.

Centering prayer stands in a long tradition of "mantric" meditation, where a psalm is chanted or a phrase is repeated over and over, as in the Jesus Prayer, to center on the Divine. The difference found in centering prayer is that the word or phrase is not fixed but fluid. It may change from time to time.

For help with this prayer form, see *Open Mind, Open Heart* (1986), by Thomas Keating.

RECALLING GOD

In the midst of very busy days and hectic schedules, it is not easy to maintain our awareness of God and our communion with holy mystery. One way to "catch our breath," the breath of God's Holy Spirit within us, is to program ourselves with a little exercise of taking time out at intervals during the day just to *stop* and simply remember God in that brief moment of interrupting business as usual.

Try this discipline recommended by Lanza del Vasto: Stop what you are doing three times in the morning and three times in the afternoon, at intervals of two hours. *Don't do anything.*

For half a minute, just recall God's presence, sense God's love, enjoy God's creation. Breathe deeply; go inward into your self; make room in your outer routine and your inner being for God to speak. Not every break in the routine will bring a revelation of God. It will, at very least, though, bring renewed perspective to whatever it is you are doing at the time. Everyone has thirty seconds in two hours simply to be open to a sense of the sacred.

For help with this spiritual discipline, see *Make Straight the Way of the Lord,* by Lanza del Vasto (del Vasto, 1, 27–28).

ATTENTION: LOOKING WITH THE EYES OF LOVE

Loving attention is different from the previous exercise because it is an ongoing way of relating to the world. Like "recalling God," it is practiced not in isolation from what one is doing but rather in the midst of everything one is doing. It is an immersion in both the loving presence of God and the loving of the world that flows from God.

Loving attention means a double awareness of what one is doing. It requires being aware of the activity in which one is engaged and aware of oneself as one engages in the activity. It is not just doing something with careful attention but being conscious of one's inner attitudes of compassion or hatred, gentleness or violence, patience or annoyance, hope or despair. The intent of this discipline is to do everything out of the loving energy of God that flows through us. When one becomes aware of the places where this energy is blocked (with hatred, violence, annoyance, despair), one is able to transform one's inner attitude and reform one's outer action.

A variation of this discipline is called "seeing through peaceful eyes" and is particularly dedicated to relationships with other people. In the course of one's day, at work, in the family, with friends, with strangers, one holds inside a deep respect for the other person. One asks, "Why are you hurting?" One meets the other person with a loving intent and prayerfulness that acknowledge our common humanity and celebrate our mutual divinity as beloved people created in the image of God.

For help with this spiritual discipline, see *Practicing the Presence of God,* by Brother Lawrence (1962); *How You Can Be a Peacemaker*

(1985), by Mary Evelyn Jegen; and *Waiting for God,* by Simone Weil (Weil, 7, 105–16).

In providing these suggestions, we hope that the reader will find the gleanings more than just helpful and inspiring thoughts. We hope that the reader will use them as a beginning point of prayer and for a more spiritually focused life. We intend them to be kindling for the fire of God's Spirit to burn brightly in the reader's daily activity and relationships. We hope that the gleanings we have offered and these practical helps for spiritual formation will nurture a spiritual life that is not a life apart from the world but a life together with all God's people. Words of Meister Eckhart again make this point: "If a person were in a rapture as great as St. Paul once experienced and learned that a neighbor were in need of a cup of soup, it would be best to withdraw from the rapture and give the person the soup she needs."[3]

Biographical and Bibliographical Essay

Who are these women and men from whom we have been gleaning? They are those "who wore at their hearts the fire's centre . . . and left the vivid air signed with their honour" (Spender).[1]

In the pages that follow, we have provided brief sketches about the writers included here, with a few facts about each of their lives. When appropriate, we draw attention to some points that bear on their work as "spiritually centered" writers. We also make occasional reference to connections that suggest some common aim that sets this century of writers apart.

There is a special weave among many of these writers—as if they are in intimate and urgent conversation with one another. Some were, in fact, personally tied to one another: These include Thomas Merton, William Stringfellow, and Daniel Berrigan concerning issues of war and peace and biblical social conscience; Karl Barth and Dietrich Bonhoeffer concerning the German church struggle during Adolf Hitler's rise to power; Franz Rosenzweig and Martin Buber in stimulating the Jewish renaissance in Europe after World War I. Barth and Hans Urs von Balthasar were colleagues in Basel for many years and held conversations on both doctrinal and faith issues.

Some of these writers knew of others from whom we have gleaned because of the special interest their writings or their lives had for them: for example, the writings of Pierre Teilhard de Chardin and Simone Weil stimulated the religious reflections of Flannery O'Connor, and Thomas Merton thought that Alexander Schmemann was the best theologian he had read for years. Václav Havel, while in prison, was sent hand-copied essays of Emmanuel Levinas, which strongly shaped his thinking about human responsibility. Maggie Ross is the translator and editor of the talks of "A Carthusian" of the Grand Chartreuse Abbey, and he, in turn, echoes some of Thomas Merton's spirit. Evelyn Underhill's writings on mysticism earlier in the century seemed to open new avenues of thought for many of our authors. Few of our chosen writers were actually "mystics"; those who were called mystics were Pierre Teilhard de Chardin, Simone Weil, and Dag Hammarskjöld.

There are other links, too. Some were discussed in the thematic development of "directional guidelines" in our introductory essay. The last connection we will mention before sketching each author's life and spiritually centered writings is that between *contemplation* and *action*. Some of our readers will recognize how an incarnational thread runs through Simone Weil, Dietrich Bonhoeffer, Dorothy Day, Martin Luther King Jr., William Stringfellow, Daniel Berrigan, Mother Teresa of Calcutta, and Václav Havel, compelling each of them to "radical" courses of action in the world. Their actions had profoundly transforming consequences within particular times and places. These actions, all would say, were not of their doing; rather, they were signs of grace, of a spirit of holiness working through their lives. Such actions were the direct consequence of their conscious contemplative spirit drawing God into their lives so that a sense of the sacred could be visible through them.

HANS URS VON BALTHASAR (1905–1988)

Von Balthasar's theology is best known for its focus on doctrines of the Trinity and on the emphasis of beauty and holiness in the Christian faith. During his early life in Switzerland, he was a free-lance writer and journalist; after the Second World War, his theological teaching and writing developed steadily. He became the central theologian of the Catholic faculty at Basel. There, as a contemporary of Karl Barth, he engaged in many interfaith dialogues and found his theology and Barth's to complement each other, especially in their focus on Christology. Although he is not as well known in Catholic circles as Karl Rahner or Hans Küng, his influence is increasing as the twentieth century winds down. Of note among his more spiritual writings is *The Heart of the World* (1946). We have gleaned from:

1. *The von Balthasar Reader.* Edited by Medard Kehl, S.J., and Werner Löser, S.J. New York: Crossroad, 1982.

KARL BARTH (1886–1968)

Few would dispute that Karl Barth was the leading Protestant theologian of the twentieth century. He began his pastoral career in 1909 in Geneva and ended his career as a professor at the University of Basel. Much of the period between the world wars was spent teaching in Germany (at Göttingen, Münster, and Bonn). Before taking up the writing of his great *Church Dogmatics* (begun in the early 1930s and not quite completed at his death in 1968), Barth had changed the course of twentieth-century theology from its nineteenth-century "liberal" orientation with the publication in 1919 of his commentary *The Epistle to the Romans.* This book ushered in what has been called crisis theology, with some existentialist themes from Søren Kierkegaard evident. It began what has been called in our century neo-orthodox theology, wherein God's grace and mystery come to us through God's Word, radically incarnated in the gospel of Jesus Christ. This was the basis on which Barth prepared the draft of the famous Barmen Declaration of the Confessing Church of Germany in 1934. The Barmen Declaration affirmed that the lordship of Christ was not to be shared by any principality or power, especially not the Third Reich. The Word of God was sovereign over the laws of the state. Barth's role at Barmen and subsequent denunciation of Nazism (his refusal to take an oath of allegiance to the Führer) forced his return to Switzerland in 1935.

Barth's main theological task was to guide theology back to the prophetic teaching of the Bible and away from a natural religious philosophy. This was done by a radical refocusing on Christology, on the imminence of God as manifested in God's Word in Jesus Christ to the world. It is through this christological emphasis that Barth provides us with a spiritually based message that resonates throughout his writing and preaching. Barth's works from which we have gleaned are:

1. *Church Dogmatics*. Vol. I, *The Doctrine of the Word of God,* part 2. Edinburgh: T. & T. Clark, 1956.
2. *Church Dogmatics*. Vol. III, *The Doctrine of Creation,* part 2. Edinburgh: T. & T. Clark, 1960.
3. *Church Dogmatics*. Vol. IV, *The Doctrine of Reconciliation,* Part 1. Edinburgh: T. & T. Clark, 1961.
4. *Evangelical Theology: An Introduction*. New York: Holt, Rinehart & Winston, 1963.
5. *The German Church Conflict*. Richmond: John Knox Press, 1965.
6. *God Here and Now. Religious Perspectives*. Vol. 9. New York: Harper & Row, 1964.
7. *A Karl Barth Reader*. Edited by Rolf Joachim Erler and Reiner Marquard. Grand Rapids: Wm. B. Eerdmans Publishing Co., 1986.

DANIEL BERRIGAN (b. 1921)

Daniel Berrigan is priest, poet, and political activist. He is best known for using his many talents as a kind of "monastic witness." He is a cofounder of both the Catholic Peace Fellowship (1964) and Clergy and Laity Concerned about Vietnam (1965).

His greatest notoriety came in May 1968, when he and eight others, including his brother and fellow priest Philip Berrigan, burned draft files with homemade napalm at Draft Board 33 in Catonsville, Maryland. In 1970, while a fugitive from "justice" (see his *The Dark Night of Resistance*), Daniel Berrigan took sanctuary at the Block Island, Rhode Island, home of William Stringfellow. There began a fifteen-year friendship between the two. His trial and defense are chronicled in his *The Trial of the Catonsville Nine* (1970), which won the Obie Drama Award and the Los Angeles Drama Critics Award in 1971.

Berrigan was and is active against all forms of violence: the Vietnam War, nuclear arms development, the arms race, revolutionary violence, violence to children and the unborn. For this activism he has been in and out of prison for over two decades. At the end of the 1970s, when asked how many times he had been arrested, he said, "As yet, not enough." This period culminated in his arrest in 1980 as part of the Ploughshares Eight group, who "symbolically struck a blow" to nuclear arms construction at the General Electric assembly plant in King of Prussia, Pennsylvania, when they poured blood on a missile's nose-cone. During the past decade, Berrigan has been working with the poor and victims of HIV (human immunodeficiency virus) in New York City.

All of these "radical" activities would be hollow were it not for Berrigan's life of prayer and his unswerving commitment to the commandment "Thou shalt not kill." Prayer and pacifism have been at the center of this man's life; they are the motivation for his passionate witness to what he believes to be the truth and the spirit of the gospel of Christ. His works from which we have gleaned are:

1. *The Dark Night of Resistance.* New York: Bantam Books, 1972.
2. *Ten Commandments for the Long Haul.* Nashville: Abingdon Press, 1981.
3. *Uncommon Prayer: A Book of Psalms.* New York: Seabury Press, 1978.
4. *Sorrow Built a Bridge: Friendship and AIDS.* Baltimore: Fortkamp, 1989.

(We note also his autobiography, *To Dwell in Peace* [1987], and several books of his poems: *False Gods, Real Men* [1969]; *Selected and New Poems* [1973]; *Prison Poems* [1973]; and *Daniel Berrigan: Poetry, Drama, Prose* [1988].)

ANTHONY BLOOM (b. 1914)

In 1966 Anthony Bloom became Metropolitan Anthony of Sourozh; and since 1962 he has been Archbishop in charge of the Russian Orthodox Patriarchal Church in Great Britain and Ireland. He is well known to British audiences through his many talks and his books on prayer.

Metropolitan Anthony of Sourozh was born in Lausanne, Switzerland. His childhood was spent in Russia and Persia, his father being a member of the Russian imperial diplomatic corps. His family had to leave Persia during the revolution and came to Paris, where Anthony was educated. He received degrees in physics, chemistry, and biology and a doctorate in medicine at the University of Paris. During World War II he served as an officer in the French army until the fall of France. He then worked as a surgeon in one of the Paris hospitals and also took part in the Resistance. In 1943 he professed monastic vows while practicing medicine in Paris. He was ordained a priest in the Russian Orthodox Church in 1948, and in 1949 he went to England as Orthodox chaplain to the Fellowship of St. Alban and St. Sergius. He rose steadily to the rank of metropolitan through his service in England.

Metropolitan Anthony's writings are much loved, especially for his gift in telling stories that come from his many encounters with people throughout the world—ranging from his patients when he was a physician to national leaders and theologians. We have gleaned from four of his more popular writings:

1. *Beginning to Pray.* New York: Paulist Press, 1970. (This was also published under the title *School for Prayer;* London: Darton, Longman & Todd, 1970.)
2. *Creative Prayer: Daily Readings with Metropolitan Anthony of Sourozh.* Introduced and selected by Hugh Wybrew. London: Darton, Longman & Todd, 1987.
3. *God and Man.* New York: Paulist Press, 1971.
4. *Meditations: A Spiritual Journey through the Parables.* Denville, N.J.: Dimension Books, 1972.

DIETRICH BONHOEFFER (1906–1945)

It is difficult not to provide a longer account than follows of Bonhoeffer's life and death. Although considered by many as a leading Protestant theologian (Karl Barth hailed his doctoral dissertation of 1927, *Sanctorum Communio,* as a "theological miracle"), he was best known as Pastor Bonhoeffer. From early in the rise of the Third Reich, Bonhoeffer resisted its anti-Semitism and, like Barth, stood strongly as a "confessing" Christian, refusing loyalty to the state over the lordship of Jesus Christ. For several years in the mid-to-late 1930s, Bonhoeffer ran an illegal underground Confessing Church seminary in Finkenwalde. After the war began, Bonhoeffer, through family connections, infiltrated the German army as part of the German resistance movement and from within it plotted to overthrow Hitler and work for peace. He ultimately conspired as part of the *Abwehr* resistance circle that attempted to assassinate Hitler. For this he was arrested by the gestapo in 1943 and imprisoned until he was tried and hanged in April 1945, just days before U.S. troops liberated his concentration camp at Flossenbürg.

Bonhoeffer's story is surely one of the most significant in our century for hard ethical and spiritual reflection; it raises the most difficult and most profound issues regarding the "cost of discipleship," responsibility to one's neighbor, the dangers of nationalism, and the importance of community. In his books, essays, letters, and poems, Bonhoeffer offers prayerful, pastoral, and critical reflection on all of these issues and more. For example, few have recognized the degree to which his writings reflect themes similar to those of liberation theology, associated with a later time and linked with Latin American Catholic Christians. In one essay, addressed to fellow conspirators, he writes that they have "learned to see the great events of world history from below, from the perspective of the outcast, the suspects, the maltreated, the powerless, the oppressed, the reviled—in short, from the perspective of those who suffer" (*A Testament to Freedom*, xiv). His writings are perhaps among those most exemplary of the connection between contemplation and action. We have selected the following works from which to glean, realizing that there is a larger harvest untended:

1. *The Cost of Discipleship.* New York: Macmillan Co., 1959.
2. *Ethics.* New York: Macmillan Co., 1962.
3. *Letters and Papers from Prison.* Translated and introduced by John W. Doberstein. New York: Macmillan Co., Macmillan Paperbacks, 1962.
4. *Life Together.* New York: Harper & Brothers, 1954.

(We also note a new and important collection of Bonhoeffer's writings that includes many difficult-to-find essays and poems, in addition to selections from major works: *A Testament to Freedom: The Essential Writings of Dietrich Bonhoeffer*, ed. Geffrey B. Kelly and F. Burton Nelson [HarperSanFrancisco, 1990].)

MARTIN BUBER (1878–1965)

Buber earned his doctoral degree at the University of Vienna in 1904 with a thesis on German mysticism. This complemented his already deep interest in the Jewish tradition of Hasidism. Buber lifted up Hasidic teachings through the retelling of the tradition's stories and the publishing of its literature. With the rise of the Third Reich he was no longer allowed to teach in German universities, and he resigned his university post at Frankfurt and became the director of the Frankfurter Jüdische Lehrhaus. He had been deeply involved with Jewish religious education from early in the century right up to the beginning of World War II and, with Franz Rosenzweig, was credited with stimulating what was called the Jewish renaissance—the reawakening of the great philosophical and religious traditions of his people. This reawakening certainly helped Jews keep their faith through the trials that lay ahead. From 1938 to 1951 Buber was on the faculty of the Hebrew University in Jerusalem. For a number of years after his retirement he lectured in the United States.

Buber is considered the embodiment of the ancient Zaddik tradition, that of the rabbis or "perfect men" who were teachers, who brought the word of God to the common person. They were considered the unifying forces and spiritual leaders of the Jewish communities. Buber served as an interpreter of modern Jewish thought to the non-Jewish world. His theology falls into the general movement of religious existentialism. It strives for a dialogue between God and human beings, where both are addressed with the personal, holy "I" and "Thou" in the relationship. This is outlined in his best-known philosophical book, *I and Thou* (1937, 1958, repr. 1987). We have gleaned from the following works of Buber:

1. *A Believing Humanism: Gleanings.* New York: Simon & Schuster, 1969.
2. *Daniel: Dialogues on Realization.* New York: McGraw-Hill Book Co., 1964.
3. *Paths in Utopia.* Boston: Beacon Press, 1949.
4. *The Writings of Martin Buber.* Selected and edited by Will Herberg. New York: Meridian Books, 1956.

DOM HELDER CAMARA (b. 1909)

Dom Helder Camara was ordained a priest in 1931, and in 1952 he was consecrated a bishop, serving in Rio de Janeiro. He was archbishop of Olinda and Recife in northeastern Brazil from 1964 to 1984. Dom Helder played a major role during the Second Vatican

Council (1962–1965), where he organized informal meetings with bishops from around the world who shared his concern that the church be a church of the poor, a servant church. By the end of the council, his group came to exert great influence on Pope Paul VI.

Dom Helder has always been a champion of the poor and advocate of nonviolent social change. He was greatly influenced by Gandhi and Martin Luther King Jr. and is theologically indebted to Teilhard de Chardin. He was twice nominated for the Nobel Peace Prize as he stood firmly against the repression of the Brazilian peasants by the ruling military junta. In 1970 he received the Martin Luther King Jr. International Peace Prize.

He is a simple man, totally available to the people of all classes who flock to him literally day and night. His spiritual legacy is found most clearly in his "Meditations," written between 2:00 and 4:00 A.M. every morning since his seminary days. These meditations have been translated into many languages. Poetic in form, profound in content, deceptively simple in diction, they are unique in the treasury of Christian spirituality.[2] Gleanings are from:

1. *Hoping against All Hope.* Maryknoll, N.Y.: Orbis Books, 1984.
2. *Into Your Hands, Lord.* Oak Park, Ill.: Meyer-Stone Books, 1987.
3. *Sister Earth: Ecology and the Spirit.* London: New City, 1990.

(We also refer you to *The Desert Is Fertile* [1976] and *A Thousand Reasons for Living* [1981].)

A CARTHUSIAN OF THE ABBEY OF GRAND CHARTREUSE

We know little of who this monk is, but an Anglican solitary, Maggie Ross, has translated his rich teachings from conferences with his novices and brought them to our attention in *The Way of Silent Love.* There are additional volumes in the making. From the translator's preface we know only that this Carthusian thought these conferences "highly personal." As "Father Master," he holds up his teachings "before God in prayer" and sees them as worth only what his own love is worth. We have gleaned from this one published book, as well as from translations of further, unpublished conferences made available to the authors by the translator (and used with her permission):

1. *The Way of Silent Love: Carthusian Novice Conferences.* Translated by an Anglican solitary. Kalamazoo, Mich.: Cistercian Publications, 1993.

DOROTHY DAY (1897–1980)

Dorothy Day began her life of faith at the age of eight at a Methodist Sunday school. During her high school years, she was moved by the plight of the poor and became involved in issues of peace and justice. This commitment lasted for the rest of her life and included the anti-draft movement during World War I and also suffrage issues. After the war she was a writer for a time and in 1927 converted to Roman Catholicism.

When she returned to New York, she met Peter Maurin, whose ideas would dominate the rest of her life. With him, she founded *The Catholic Worker,* which encouraged the use of love to change institutions and improve human life. On May 1, 1933, in Union Square, Day hawked the first issue of *The Catholic Worker.* In her book *From Union Square to Rome* (1938), Day told of her conversion to Christianity. In 1952 she published her autobiography, *The Long Loneliness,* which chronicled her struggle with Catholic priests whose vision of life did not extend beyond their parish.

Dorothy Day's life was one of commitment and compassion. She was perhaps best known by those who visited her in the 1950s and 1960s at the Catholic Workers House in lower Manhattan, where she lived and worked until the day she died in 1980. Her personal influence on religious activists and writers such as Thomas Merton, William Stringfellow, and Daniel Berrigan was profound. We have gleaned from:

1. *The Long Loneliness: The Autobiography of Dorothy Day.* San Francisco: Harper & Row, 1952.

LANZA DEL VASTO (1901–1981)

Born in San Vito dei Normanni, Italy, Lanza del Vasto is descended from an illustrious family that can count among its members emperors of the West and Norman kings of Sicily. He learned several languages as a child and eventually pursued a doctorate in philosophy at the University of Pisa.

In 1936 he journeyed across India, mostly on foot. In India he began to combine the essence of both Eastern religions and his own Catholicism. As World War II was coming to an end, several people sought him out to help form a small group in Paris that would have its basis in living life simply. The first rural community, which became a formal communal order, was formed in Tournier in 1948. Called "The Ark" (L'Arche), it was open to all and dedicated to implanting love and truth. It chose spinning, weaving, and farming as a communal way of life but went into the world practicing nonviolent resistance in the face of such issues as French nuclear testing and the war in Algeria. The community soon moved to Bollene, and in 1963 it moved again to Borie Noble. The Ark community now is made up of several communities and it promotes and practices nonviolence on all levels.

Del Vasto's simple life, his pacifism, and his ready maxims have been an inspiration to many people throughout the world. We have gleaned from three works:

1. *Make Straight the Way of the Lord.* New York: Alfred A. Knopf, 1974.
2. *Principles and Precepts of the Return to the Obvious.* New York: Schocken Books, 1974.
3. *Return to the Source.* New York: Schocken Books, 1972. (This account of his encounter with Gandhi and his Indian spiritual pilgrimage was published in France in 1943 and became a best-selling book.)

CATHERINE DE HUECK DOHERTY (1896–1985)

Catherine de Hueck Doherty was born on August 15, 1896, in Nijni-Novgorod, Russia. She attended the University of Petrograd and emigrated to Canada in 1921. After leaving Russia she made her living as a waitress, salesclerk, and factory worker, and for a decade or more as a lecturer and manager at a lecture bureau in New York City. In 1943 she married Edward Doherty.

Catherine and her husband dedicated their lives to helping the poor. In Toronto she founded the first Friendship House. Others would soon follow in the United States: in Harlem (New York City),

Chicago, Washington, D.C., and Portland, Oregon. In 1947 she and her husband formed Madonna House, a place for friendship, prayer, and simple love—one that, as a follower of hers has said, holds up "a vision of cosmic tenderness."

We have gleaned from one of her writings that has become a modern spiritual classic. A coworker at Madonna House wrote, "Those of us who have been touched by the fire of God within her . . . pray that each person who reads this book will touch that same fire. May the risen Lord lead each of you into the desert of your heart, and speak to you there in his Spirit. . . . Then, may he lead you to his brothers and sisters who are everywhere awaiting your love" (Doherty, 1, 14). Although Doherty was brought up a Roman Catholic, she draws heavily on her Russian background and incorporates ideas and practices from Eastern Orthodox desert spirituality, making them available for everyday use.

1. *Poustinia: Christian Spirituality of the East for Western Man.* Glasgow: Fontana Books, 1977.

MATTHEW FOX (b. 1940)

Matthew Fox joined the Dominicans (Order of Friars Preachers) in 1960 and was ordained a priest in 1967. His writings have been on the margins of the Catholic tradition, and his Creation Spirituality, which was discussed in our Introduction, has had a mixed reception within the church. While generally regarded as outside the bounds of orthodoxy, it has certainly spawned a strong "alternative" spirituality among both Catholics and non-Catholics. Creation Spirituality is a product of the 1960s countercultural revolution and it has spoken to many persons who have not wanted to affiliate with institutionalized religion but who nevertheless seek a lifestyle that embraces the sacred in life. Matthew Fox's writings flow easily between medieval mysticism and Native American spirituality. We have gleaned from:

1. *On Becoming a Musical Mystical Bear.* New York: Paulist Press, 1972.
2. *The Coming of the Cosmic Christ.* San Francisco: Harper & Row, 1988.

GUSTAVO GUTIÉRREZ (b. 1928)

Gustavo Gutiérrez's name is nearly synonymous with liberation theology in its very best sense. His book *A Theology of Liberation* (1972) has provided the foundation for all subsequent reflection in that area. His theological views and writings come from his work with the poor in Rica, a slum in Lima, Peru, and from his reflections with other Latin American priests on the church's relationship to the rich and poor in Latin America. Bishops' conferences at Medellín, Colombia, and Puebla, Mexico, have provided the practical and ecclesiastical framework for liberation theology, and Gutiérrez has given it its theological shape.

Gutiérrez was born in Lima, Peru, and educated there and in Europe. He was ordained a priest in 1959. He is professor of theology at the Catholic University in Lima and adviser to the National Union of Catholic Students. In 1982 Henri Nouwen attended a course offered by Gutiérrez in Lima. He writes of that experience in the Foreword to *We Drink from Our Own Wells:* "Gustavo's spirituality came alive for me precisely through those who were receiving it with open mind and eager heart"; it was a spirituality of liberation touching every dimension of life, "a truly biblical spirituality that allows God's saving act in history to penetrate all levels of human existence" (Gutiérrez 2, xv). "Gustavo stressed the importance of warm, affectionate, and caring relationships among those who struggle for and with the poor" (Gutiérrez 2, xvii). We have gleaned from two works by Gutiérrez that develop his spirituality of liberation:

1. *A Theology of Liberation.* Maryknoll, N.Y.: Orbis Books, 1972.
2. *We Drink from Our Own Wells: the Spiritual Journey of a People.* Maryknoll, N.Y.: Orbis Books, 1984.

DAG HAMMARSKJÖLD (1905–1961)

Dag Hammarskjöld was born on July 29, 1905, in Jönköping, Sweden. He studied at Uppsala University, where he received his B.A. in 1925, his M.A. in 1928, and his LL.B. in 1930. He earned his Ph.D. at Stockholm University in 1934. He became secretary-general of the United Nations in 1953 and died in a plane crash in Zambia while trying to bring peace to the Congo. Almost all of his life was spent in diplomatic service in Sweden and in the United Nations.

It came as a big surprise to his colleagues in the world community when a manuscript of *Markings* was found in Hammarskjöld's New York apartment after his death. He had called this "a sort of a White Book concerning my negotiations with myself—and with God." Part of *Markings* reflects what he refers to as his "journey inwards"—a journey he also called the "longest"—as well as his interest in Jesus' own fellowship with God, in the writings of mystics (especially Meister Eckhart and Thomas à Kempis), and in the Psalms as the driving force of his lifework. With such a revelation as to what was driving this man of peace, who had no apparent "religious" or "church" affiliation nor any desire to find one, it does not seem odd to identify him with the long tradition of mystical writers. Hammarskjöld wrote in *Markings*, "For many of us in this era the road to holiness necessarily passes through the world of action." This combination of contemplation and action is very characteristic of those who seek to deepen their life in the spirit; when they do so, the "action" seems necessarily to follow. A good portion of *Markings* consists of poems, some in haiku form. We have not gleaned from the poetry.

1. *Markings*. New York: Alfred A. Knopf, 1966.

VÁCLAV HAVEL (b. 1936)

Václav Havel is one of the truly remarkable human beings of our century. His unassuming manner, his passion to tell the truth, and his unswerving commitment to the human drive for freedom are astonishing. There are many parallels between Havel and Martin Luther King Jr. in terms of dedication to human and civil rights. Each sought to realize freedom and justice for his people in a situation where such freedom and justice had been denied and suppressed; both engaged in a continual struggle to align his "religious" or "spiritual" beliefs with specific concrete actions. King used his prophetic skills and the platform of the church to shape the American civil rights movement, while Havel used his literary skill and his tenacity and compassion to direct a human rights movement and reshape the life of his country, Czechoslovakia.

After completion of his compulsory education in 1951, Havel's literary and university aspirations were denied him by the Czech Communist regime, in part because of his aristocratic family background. He was channeled through a series of technical schools and jobs but continued to write, and by 1956 he had begun to speak out for new writers' freedoms. After his two-year military service, Havel began a long association with theater groups around Prague, as stage technician and scriptwriter. The theater became a platform from which Havel could speak indirectly about the conditions in which the Czech people had to live under their Communist regime. Through the success of his plays, Havel was also being noticed in the theater world in Western Europe and America.

He married Olga Splichalova in 1964, and from that point through the Prague Spring uprising of 1968 and on to the Charter 77 movement, Havel's voice, among others, grew clearer and stronger regarding the need of human beings for freedom and dignity, and the inability of citizens to live a life in truth amid the lies and deception of their leaders and the state bureaucracy.

There are many fine points in Havel's journey to his founding role in the Charter 77 movement, but the short of it is that this public declaration of principles of freedom and human dignity led to Havel's arrest, a series of trials, and imprisonment for the next seven or eight years, through 1985. We have gleaned from two books of collected essays and letters written between 1975 and 1985. These essays and letters provide a very personal account of Václav Havel's sense of purpose and his struggle to connect "God," or what he prefers to call the "absolute horizon of Being," with a sense of responsibility to love his neighbors to the point of liberating them and restoring their dignity.

Havel—together with many other Czech citizens—was successful in his cause. In 1989 the "velvet revolution" took place, led by Havel. Without a shot fired, the Czech Communist government (in the face of thousands of people holding vigil in the streets) resigned, free elections were held, and in 1990 Havel was elected president of the new democratic government of Czechoslovakia by a landslide, serving until mid-1992. After Czechoslovakia divided into two separate states in 1993, Havel was elected president of the Czech Republic.

1. *Letters to Olga: June 1979–September 1982.* New York: Henry Holt & Co., Owl Books, 1989.
2. *Living in Truth.* London and Boston: Faber & Faber, 1989.

(Among Havel's better-known plays translated into English are *The Memorandum* [1967], performed at the New York Shakespeare Festival in 1968; *The Increased Difficulty of Concentration* [1972]; *A Butterfly on the Aerial* [1975]; an adaptation of *The Beggar's Opera* [1975]; *Conversation* [1978]; *Mistake* [1984]; and *Temptation* [1988], performed in London and New York in recent years.)

ABRAHAM JOSHUA HESCHEL (1907–1972)

Born in Warsaw, Poland, Heschel was the son and grandson of Hasidic rabbis who themselves were descended from talmudic scholars as far back as the sixteenth century. In 1933 he received his Ph.D. from the University of Berlin. During the 1930s he was an instructor of the Talmud in a number of Jewish schools in Germany and Poland.

In 1938 Heschel was expelled from Germany, and he fled Poland just two months before the Nazi invasion. In 1940 he began teaching in Jewish reform circles and at the Hebrew Union College at Cincinnati, where in 1943 he took the position of assistant professor of Jewish philosophy and rabbinics. Then in 1945 he became a professor of Jewish ethics and mysticism at the Jewish Theological Seminary of America.

Heschel's style is fresh and unsystematic, and he is always searching for ways to help the ordinary person grasp God and participate in the holiness of life. In his later years he talked about his insights and related them to concrete problems such as prayer, symbolism, youth, aging, racial justice, civil rights, interfaith dialogue, and the state of Israel. We have gleaned passages from his best known and most comprehensive work:

1. *God in Search of Man: A Philosophy of Judaism.* San Francisco: Harper & Row, Harper Torchbooks, 1966.

POPE JOHN XXIII (1881–1963)

Angelo Giuseppe Roncalli was the oldest son in a family of thirteen children. His father was a poor tenant farmer. He was ordained a priest in 1904, served as a chaplain through World War I, and entered the diplomatic service of the Vatican State in 1925. He rose in the ranks from bishop to cardinal (1953).

He was best known as a pastor and simple priest and he seemed, of all the cardinals through the 1950s, to be the least political and thus unlikely at his age to do anything dramatic. When Pope Pius XII died in 1958, Giuseppe Roncalli, at age seventy-seven, was elected pope. Some considered his election to be that of caretaker or transitional pope. But from his first day in office, he set off a revolution in the Roman Catholic Church that is still sending shock waves through the church on every continent.

His most important move was to call an Ecumenical Council of Bishops (the first since 1870) to reform almost every aspect of the church. He died during the second session of the Second Vatican Council in 1963. During his short time as pope, he issued eight encyclical letters, all of which were pastoral and spiritual in tone and provided an impetus for the reforms that took place through the council. We have gleaned from two of his encyclical letters:

1. *Mater et Magistra* (Christianity and Social Progress), Glen Rock, N.J.: Paulist Press, 1961.
2. *Pacem in Terris* (Peace on Earth). Washington, D.C.: National Catholic Welfare Conference, 1963.

MARTIN LUTHER KING JR. (1929–1968)

Recognized as the driving force behind the American civil rights movement of the 1950s and 1960s, Dr. Martin Luther King Jr. should also be recognized for his brilliance as an orator, writer, and peacemaker. These gifts came together around his clear religious convictions and were shaped by his passion for love and justice for all humanity.

He entered Morehouse College at the age of fifteen and earned his B.A. in 1948. He was persuaded by his Morehouse teachers to enter

Crozer Theological Seminary in Pennsylvania. At Crozer he was exposed to the teachings of Mahatma Gandhi and Walter Rauschenbusch. In his senior year he read Rauschenbusch's *Christianity and the Social Crisis* (1913), which asserted that the church must work to undo social injustices. It was Gandhi's philosophy of nonviolence and returning good for evil that King made a part of his own strategy to fight against injustice and racism.

As a pastor in Montgomery, Alabama, in 1955 King was elected president of the Montgomery Improvement Association and led the protest in support of Rosa Parks's refusal to give up her seat to a white person on a bus. He organized a bus boycott that lasted more than a year. Despite threatening phone calls and the bombing of his house, the boycott was successful. In 1959, the U.S. Supreme Court declared Montgomery's segregation laws unconstitutional. Soon after, King was made president of the Southern Christian Leadership Conference. Its goal was to enlarge black voter registration and eliminate segregation in the South.

At the end of 1962 King decided to focus his energy on desegregating Birmingham, Alabama, because he considered it the South's most segregated city. It was here that he wrote his famous "Letter from Birmingham City Jail," setting forth his justification for his involvement in Birmingham's human affairs.

In 1963 King led a massive march on the nation's capital. It was here that he gave the speech that still resonates in our hearts, which concluded with these lines: "I have a dream that one day on the red hills of Georgia the sons of former slaves and the sons of former slaveowners will be able to sit down together at the table of brotherhood. . . . I have a dream that my four little children will one day live in a nation where they will not be judged by the color of their skin but by the content of their character."[3]

King was given the Nobel Peace Prize in 1964. He was the twelfth American, the third African American, and at thirty-five, the youngest person ever to win the prize. From 1964 until his assassination in 1968, King kept alive the struggle against poverty and for human justice with love, and he persisted with his nonviolent philosophy as he opposed U.S. involvement in the war in Vietnam. In 1967 he worked in the Poverty Coalition (Poor People's Campaign). He was assassinated on April 4, 1968, in Memphis, Tennessee, where he had gone to lead a march in solidarity with striking sanitation workers.

We have gleaned passages from just three of his speeches and essays (only one of which is widely known) to illustrate the connection between his deeply centered spirituality and his commitment to human justice. These particular pieces express his sense of a universal spirituality.

1. *Beyond Vietnam: A Prophecy for the '80's.* New York: Clergy and Laity Concerned, 1982.
2. *Letter from Birmingham City Jail.* Philadelphia: American Friends Service Committee, May 1963.
3. "My Pilgrimage to Nonviolence," *Stride Toward Freedom: The Montgomery Story.* New York: Harper & Brothers, 1958.

(We refer you to one group of King's writings, a collection of sermons of particular relevance to his spirituality: *Strength to Love* [1963; Philadelphia: Fortress Press, 1981].)

MADELEINE L'ENGLE (b. 1918)

Throughout her childhood Madeleine L'Engle enjoyed writing, drawing, and playing the piano. When her family moved from the United States to Europe, she was sent to a strict Swiss boarding school. Eventually she returned and attended Smith College, graduating in 1941. She has taught at the University of Indiana and at St. Hilda's and St. Hugh's School, New York. In 1966 she became librarian at the Cathedral of St. John the Divine, and in 1976 she became a member of the board of directors for the Authors' League Foundation and president of the Authors' Guild of America.

L'Engle's most famous and highly praised novel, *A Wrinkle in Time* (1962), was rejected by several publishers because it was very unusual for a children's book. It won the Newbery Medal in 1963.

Some recurring themes can be found in all of L'Engle's books. There is always a conflict between good and evil, and she explores the problem of differentiating one from the other. She also has written about the nature of God, the dangers of conformity, and the necessity of giving love. Through her children's books, fiction, and the pieces from which we have gleaned, L'Engle challenges us to grasp "the creative power of love," to discipline our lives between work and prayer, and to live joyfully.

1. *And It Was Good: Reflections on Beginnings.* Wheaton, Ill.: Harold Shaw Publishers, 1983. (First in a trilogy with 5 and 4 on this list.)
2. *A Circle of Quiet.* New York: Farrar, Straus & Giroux, 1972.
3. *The Irrational Season.* New York: Seabury Press, 1977.
4. *Sold into Egypt: Joseph's Journey into Human Being.* Wheaton, Ill.: Harold Shaw Publishers, 1989. (Third in a trilogy.)
5. *A Stone for a Pillow.* Wheaton, Ill.: Harold Shaw Publishers, 1986. (Second in a trilogy.)
6. *Walking on Water: Reflections on Faith and Art.* Wheaton, Ill.: Harold Shaw Publishers, 1972.

EMMANUEL LEVINAS (b. 1906)

Emmanuel Levinas was born in Lithuania. His earliest memories include the death of Leo Tolstoy, being uprooted in World War I, and the 1917 Bolshevik Revolution—and his father's bookstore in Kovno. His earliest reading included the Hebrew Bible, Pushkin, Gogol, Dostoyevski, and Tolstoy; these writers led Levinas to Strasbourg to study philosophy under Charles Blondel and Maurice Pradines. He took a great interest in the philosophical debates in Europe during the late 1920s.

In the 1930s Levinas became a French citizen. When World War II broke out, he was utilized as an interpreter of Russian and German, but he was soon taken prisoner. Some of his most complex philosophical ideas were shaped during this period of captivity. Because of his war experience, Levinas wrote: "In the aftermath of Hitler's exterminations, which were able to take place in a Europe that had been evangelized for fifteen centuries, Judaism turned inward towards its origins. Up to that point, Christianity had accustomed Western Judaism to thinking of their origins as having dried up or as having been submerged under more lively tides. To find oneself a Jew in the wake of the Nazi massacres therefore meant once more taking up a position with regard to Christianity" (Levinas, 2, xiii). This he did, like many other postwar Jewish writers.

In 1957 he began contributing to the annual Talmud Colloquium of French Jewish Intellectuals. In 1967 he moved to Paris-Nanterre faculty and in 1973 to the Sorbonne. It has only been in the past decade that Levinas has emerged as both a major philosopher of the twentieth century and an important interpreter of Judaism. His writings on Judaism, from which we have gleaned our selections, reflect his links with the eastern European Jewish tradition (especially the strong tradition of Lithuanian rabbis), which also influenced the writing of Joseph B. Soloveitchik.

1. *The Levinas Reader.* Edited by Seán Hand. Oxford: Basil Blackwell, 1989.
2. *Difficult Freedom: Essays on Judaism.* Translated by Seán Hand. Baltimore: Johns Hopkins University Press, 1990.

(A recent translation of essays of Levinas that link themes and writers in twentieth-century Jewish spirituality is *Outside the Subject,* translated by Michael B. Smith [London: Athlone Press, 1993].)

C. S. LEWIS (1898–1963)

C. S. Lewis was born in Belfast, Ireland. His family was distinctly Protestant, his mother's father being a rector at Enniskillen and Dundella and her grandfather being bishop of Ossory in the Church of Ireland. Lewis's mother died in 1908, when he was ten. In his boarding school days he lost what faith he had but retained an elusive feeling of spirituality, which he came to call "Joy."

A tutor, William T. Kirkpatrick, introduced Lewis to the writings of George MacDonald. It was MacDonald's work that evoked this elusive "Joy" that Lewis so desperately searched for. It was not until middle age that he converted to Christianity and found the "Joy."

Lewis served in World War I in the Somerset Light Infantry. After the war he returned to Oxford and became a fellow and tutor at Magdalen College, a post he held from 1925 to 1954. In 1954 he was elected professor of medieval and Renaissance English at Cambridge University.

In his long and distinguished career, Lewis successfully embraced three literary genres: literary criticism and the history of literature; fiction and fantasy writing; and Christian moral and apologetic literature. *The Allegory of Love* (1936) is an early and well-known example of his literary-critical writings. His first venture into science fiction was his book *Out of the Silent Planet* (1938), the first of a trilogy. His most-loved books in this genre are the seven volumes of children's fantasy *The Chronicles of Narnia* (1950–1956).

Lewis's Christian literature, writes Paul L. Holmer, "addresses all of us where we are, faltering and stumbling, uncertain of what we should do or be. We are all open to a promise, poised for a great happiness and already eligible for the sweeping away of the shadows of guilt and disappointment" (*C. S. Lewis: The Shape of His Faith and Thought*, 21). It is a literature that has shown us the transforming power of living a virtuous life in the framework of a Christian description of the world; it has appealed to the human heart and mind of ordinary people, urging them to shape their lives through an embodiment of faith, hope, and love. The most popular of his books in this genre was *The Screwtape Letters* (1942).

Lewis married Joy Davidman Gresham in 1956. Soon thereafter, she was diagnosed with cancer. She died in 1960, and he in 1963. The recent play and film *Shadowlands* chronicles Lewis's years with Joy Gresham.

We have gleaned from a selection of his Christian literature:

1. *A Grief Observed*. New York: Bantam Books, 1961.
2. *Mere Christianity*. New York: Macmillan Co., 1952.
3. *The Problem of Pain*. New York: Macmillan Co., 1962.
4. *Surprised by Joy*. New York: Harcourt Brace Jovanovich, 1955.

(We note for further reading: A. N. Wilson, *C. S. Lewis: A Biography* [New York: Fawcett, Columbine Books, 1990]; and Paul L. Holmer, *C. S. Lewis: The Shape of His Faith and Thought* [San Francisco: Harper & Row, 1976].)

NANCY MAIRS

Nancy Mairs is a passionate questioner and storyteller. She lives in Tucson, Arizona, with her husband, George, and is presently confined by her multiple sclerosis. Her life and literature break many boundaries and defy her confinement.

Her book *Ordinary Time* chronicles her "uneasy and unrelenting state of religious faith"; it is honest about difficult questions that people have with their religious life and displays a life of personal pilgrimage. With its growing appeal to ordinary lay readers who struggle to find meaning in their lives that traditional religious faith often fails to provide, *Ordinary Time* is part of a different genre of contemporary writings under the heading of "spirituality." Mairs challenges the tradition without forsaking it. Mairs writes of her conversion from a devout New England Protestant teenager, "a bit mystically inclined," to an unorthodox, activist Catholic in the Southwest. She addresses important questions about women and the church.

Mairs's writing is truly a spirituality for the 1990s, much as is the new book by Kathleen Norris, *Dakota: A Spiritual Geography* (cited in our Introduction), and the work of Maggie Ross. These works place us at the doorstep of the twenty-first century, poised to accept a future that appears beyond our comprehension but is perhaps not beyond our control when we are equipped "spiritually."

1. *Ordinary Time: Cycles in Marriage, Faith, and Renewal.* Boston: Beacon Press, 1993.

THOMAS MERTON (1915–1968)

Thomas Merton was born to an English father and an American mother in Prades, France. He grew up in France, then attended Cambridge University in England for one year, completing his B.A and M.A. degrees at Columbia University in New York.

From early childhood he had a great love for the poetry of William Blake. He owed much of his religious orientation to Blake, along with Jacques Maritain, St. Augustine, Dante, and the twelfth-century Cistercians. He converted to Catholicism in 1938.

In 1941 Merton entered a strict Cistercian (Trappist) monastery, Our Lady of Gethsemani Abbey near Bardstown, Kentucky. He chose this order because of its reputation for solitude and rules of silence. Merton originally entered to save his soul and "become a saint," but his superiors saw other talents, and he was soon assigned to teach, research, and translate. In the twenty-seven years he spent at the monastery, he wrote almost fifty books and three hundred articles. His writings on the monastic life influenced many individuals considering religious vocations.

Merton's life, passionately told in his autobiography, *The Seven Storey Mountain* (1952), was a search for a union with God; the book has many similarities to Augustine's *Confessions*. Merton wrote on various topics, but none were of more importance to him than social justice and pacifism. His remarks on black Americans' fight for their civil rights, and on those seeking peace through nonviolent action, were among the most penetrating of the 1960s. His continual personal quest led him beyond the Western monastic tradition and into the study of Oriental monasticism, and his interest in Zen Buddhism gave him a more universal outlook on spirituality.

There is no one in our century who has shaped the landscape of spiritual writing more profoundly than Thomas Merton. His wit and passion come through in all his writings and recorded talks, many of which showed his deep commitment to the monastic life and its great importance for modern secular life.

Merton was given permission to participate in an ecumenical conference in Thailand, attended by Buddhist monks as well as Asian Cistercians, in 1968. His quest ended tragically when he was electrocuted by a fan with faulty wiring. His journey to the East is chronicled in his last writing, *The Asian Journal of Thomas Merton* (1973). We have selected from his many books the following for our gleanings:

1. *The Ascent to the Truth*. San Diego: Harcourt Brace Jovanovich, 1951.
2. *The Asian Journal of Thomas Merton*. Edited from original notebooks by Naomi Burton, Brother Patrick Hart, and James Laughlin. New York: New Directions, 1975.
3. *Conjectures of a Guilty Bystander*. Garden City, N.Y.: Doubleday & Co., 1968.
4. *Contemplation in a World of Action*. Garden City, N.Y.: Doubleday & Co., Image Books, 1973.
5. *Life and Holiness*. Garden City, N.Y.: Doubleday & Co., Image Books, 1974.
6. *New Seeds of Contemplation*. New York: New Directions, 1961.
7. *Opening the Bible*. Collegeville, Minn.: Liturgical Press, 1986.

8. *The Wisdom of the Desert.* New York: New Directions, 1951.
9. *Thoughts in Solitude: Reflections on the Spiritual Life and the Love of Solitude.* Garden City, N.Y.: Doubleday & Co., Image Books, 1958.
10. *Zen and the Birds of Appetite.* New York: New Directions, 1968.

HENRI NOUWEN (b. 1932)

Henri Nouwen was born in Nijkerk, Netherlands. He was ordained a Roman Catholic priest in 1957. He came to the United States in 1964 to continue his teaching in theology and pastoral psychology.

From 1966 to 1968 Nouwen was a visiting professor of psychology at the University of Notre Dame in Indiana. He was a staff member of the Pastoral Institute in Amsterdam from 1968 to 1969, and a member of the faculty at the Catholic Theological Institute in Utrecht from 1969 to 1970. He taught at Yale University Divinity School from 1971 to the early 1980s. The combination of clinical psychology and theology has given his writings a particularly practical appeal on such subjects as grief, welcoming, dealing with death, and prayer.

After spending a period of time in Latin America, Nouwen returned to the academic life as professor of divinity at Harvard University Divinity School from 1983 to 1985. He is now a member of the L'Arche Community in Canada. His writings on spirituality in contemporary society continue to be widely read.

We glean from the following works:

1. *The Genesee Diary.* Garden City, N.Y.: Doubleday & Co., Image Books, 1976.
2. *¡Gracias!* San Francisco: Harper & Row, 1983.
3. *Letters to Marc about Jesus.* London: Darton, Longman & Todd, 1988.
4. *The Life of the Beloved.* New York: Crossroad, 1992.
5. *The Living Reminder.* New York: Seabury Press, 1977.
6. *Making All Things New.* San Francisco: Harper & Row, 1981.
7. *Out of Solitude.* Notre Dame, Ind.: Ave Maria Press, 1974.
8. *Reaching Out: The Three Movements of the Spiritual Life.* Garden City, N.Y.: Doubleday, 1966.
9. "Rublev's Icon of the Trinity: A Reflection on the Spiritual Life." *Harvard Divinity Bulletin* 14, no. 5 (June-Aug. 1984), 8–9.

10. "A Spirituality of Peacemaking." *Harvard Divinity Bulletin* 16, no. 1 (Oct.-Nov. 1985).

11. *The Way of the Heart.* New York: Ballantine Books, 1981.

12. *With Open Hands.* Notre Dame, Ind.: Ave Maria Press, 1962.

FLANNERY O'CONNOR (1925–1964)

Flannery O'Connor spent most of her life in Georgia. Georgia and Tennessee provide the settings of most of her fiction. She started to publish her short essays, novels, and short stories in 1946. A victim of lupus, she was confined to a wheelchair for the last ten years of her life.

O'Connor was a Southerner and Roman Catholic. Her two novels and two collections of stories reveal a fascinating blend of Southern Gothic with prophecy and evangelism. She always insisted on incorporating Christian doctrinal concerns in her work and encouraged others to do the same. Themes of sin and redemption are found in her fiction, along with a heightened awareness for the comic and the grotesque.

Her first book, *Wise Blood,* was published in 1952 and immediately established her as a major fiction writer. This was followed by a novel, *The Violent Bear It Away* (1955), and her first book of short stories, *A Good Man Is Hard to Find* (1953). Her final collection of stories, *Everything That Rises Must Converge,* was published posthumously in 1965.

O'Connor carried on an active correspondence with friends and other writers—and with the occasional person who responded to one of her stories or talks given across the country. Selections from this correspondence have been published as *The Habit of Being,* which contains rich reflections on her understanding of the Catholic Christian life and how this is evidenced in her fiction. We have gleaned only from her letters and essays.

1. *The Habit of Being: Letters of Flannery O'Connor.* Selected and edited by Sally Fitzgerald. New York: Vintage Books, 1980.

2. *Mystery and Manners: Occasional Prose.* London: Faber & Faber, 1972.

KARL RAHNER (1904–1984)

Karl Rahner was perhaps this century's leading Roman Catholic theologian. His bibliography consists of more than four thousand entries. He wrote as a dogmatic theologian but also addressed philosophical, historical, pastoral, and spiritual questions. He and Karl Barth will survive as theological giants within their respective Catholic and Protestant traditions.

Rahner was born and raised in Freiburg im Breisgau, Germany. He entered the Society of Jesus in 1922, and in 1932 he was ordained a priest. Two years later he began a doctoral program in philosophy at the University of Freiburg, where he attended the seminars of Martin Heidegger. He moved to Innsbruck to take up a theological doctorate and began to teach dogmatic theology in 1937. When, in 1938, the Nazis closed the Innsbruck facility, Rahner moved to Vienna, serving at the Pastoral Institute there until 1944. In 1949 he returned to Innsbruck where he was responsible for courses on grace and the sacrament of penance, topics that engaged him for the rest of his life. Rahner played a major role in shaping the documents of the Second Vatican Council, which showed his pastoral as well as his theological skills.

In 1964 Rahner succeeded Romano Guardini as the chair of Christian *Weltanschauung* at the University of Munich. He taught at Münster from 1967 until his retirement in 1971. Three volumes of his magnum opus, *Theological Investigations*, are devoted to a "theology of the spiritual life" (volumes 3, 7, and 8). He died in 1984.

We have gleaned from the following:

1. *Encounters with Silence.* New York: Newman Press, 1960.
2. *Theological Investigations.* Vol. 3, *The Theology of the Spiritual Life.* New York: Crossroad, 1982.

BROTHER ROGER OF TAIZÉ (b. 1915)

Roger Schutz is the son of a Swiss Protestant pastor. While in secondary school he lived with a Catholic family, and this ecumenical upbringing was to signal his future calling. Schutz studied theology at Lausanne, but after a year of study, he began to doubt his choice. It was only after the near-death of his sister, when he prayed for her, that he knew the decision to study theology was right. By the summer of 1940 he had completed his theological studies, and in August he began to search for a house where he could live out a common Christian community life. After a long search he found a house for sale in the quiet Burgundy hillside village of Taizé with its small twelfth-century church.

While Roger was visiting Switzerland in November 1942, he was identified to the gestapo as one who had been helping Jewish refugees flee the Nazi regime. His home was soon occupied by the gestapo, and the refugees who had been there disappeared. After France was liberated in 1944, Roger returned to Taizé with three other men who were interested in living the communal life of which he had dreamed. The Brothers soon found themselves in charge of orphaned or unwanted boys.

During the winter of 1952–53, Brother Roger withdrew into silence and wrote the *Rule of Taizé.* At this point the community consisted mostly of Calvinists, Lutherans, and Methodists. By the 1960s, Anglicans became involved, and in 1969 the first Roman Catholic joined. The community thrives today, with over a hundred brothers who each year welcome to their hillside village thousands of pilgrims who are seeking a way of living their faith in our troubled times. The Ecumenical Community of Taizé has had special appeal to university-age women and men and a worldwide impact with its emphasis on prayer and silence, its innovative liturgy, and its commitment to peace and justice. Brother Roger's letters, prayers, and short writings have challenged thousands to live out their lives in Christian love for the sake of the poor and oppressed in our world.

We glean from some of these letters and writings:

1. *The Rule of Taizé.* Taizé, France: Les Presses de Taizé, 1968.
2. *This Day Belongs to God.* London: Faith Press, 1961.
3. *Festival.* Taizé, France: Les Presses de Taizé, 1973.
4. *Letters From Taizé,* a periodical letter.

(Brother Roger has coauthored several books with Mother Teresa of Calcutta; two recommended for further reading are: *Seeking the Heart of God: Reflections on Prayer* [New York: HarperCollins, 1993]; and *Meditations on the Way of the Cross* [New York: Pilgrim Press, 1987]. A collection of central writings of Brother Roger is published under the title *His Love Is a Fire* [Collegeville, Minn.: Liturgical Press, 1990].

FRANZ ROSENZWEIG (1886–1929)

Franz Rosenzweig was born in Cassel, Germany. From 1905 to 1907 he studied medicine at the Universities of Göttingen, Munich, and Freiburg. From 1907 to 1912 he studied modern history and philosophy at the Universities of Freiburg and Berlin.

In 1913 Rosenzweig, like many other "acculturated" European Jews, considered a conversion to Christianity but decided to remain a Jew. He worked in Jewish studies at Berlin from 1913 to 1914, and in 1916 he began an exchange of letters on Jewish and Christian theology with Eugen Rosenstock (a prominent Jew who had converted to Christianity). This correspondence, along with a series of letters concerning the founding of a Central European Jewish educational program and his book *It Is Time* (1918), was important for the development of what is known as the "Jewish renaissance." His major philosophical work, *The Star of Redemption,* was completed in 1919.

In 1922 Rosenzweig was diagnosed with amyotrophic lateral sclerosis (commonly known after the 1940s as Lou Gehrig's disease). Growing paralysis would tragically cut short his life, but the onset of the symptoms created a sense of urgency for his reforms in Jewish life and studies. Later that year, as he declined in health, his son Rafael was born. During 1923 his ability to write and speak diminished seriously. A rabbinical title was conferred on him by Leo Baeck in that year. Paralysis soon ended all movement in Rosenzweig's limbs. In 1925 he and Martin Buber collaborated on a Bible translation, but his health continued to deteriorate until his death in 1929.

The Jewish renaissance with which Rosenzweig was so closely associated was a revival of interest in the Hebrew language, the importance of keeping Torah, and the renewal of Jewish identity.

We have gleaned from the major collection of his writings edited by Nahum Glatzer:

1. *Franz Rosenzweig: His Life and Thought.* Edited by Nahum Glatzer. New York: Schocken Books, 1953.

MAGGIE ROSS (b. 1941)

An Anglican solitary, Maggie Ross writes with passion for life as viewed from the intersection of the cross and the incarnation. She spends most of her time between a basement room in an Oxford college and the wilderness of Alaska, mostly living alone, praying, and writing.

Her theological works (in the genre of kenotic theology) are very substantial and deserve greater recognition than they have received, especially her large work on "tears," *The Fountain and the Furnace: The Way of Tears and Fire.*

Like the Carthusian whom she discovered and whose conversations she has been translating for the public's benefit, there is not a lot to write about the "career" of Maggie Ross—at least, not a lot that she would wish to have made public. The most intimate portrayal of who she is and how she lives can be found in her wonderful autobiographical memoir from Alaska, *Seasons of Death and Life: A Wilderness Memoir.* We have gleaned from the following sources:

1. *The Fire of Your Life: A Solitude Shared.* New York: Paulist Press, 1983.
2. *The Fountain and the Furnace: The Way of Tears and Fire.* New York: Paulist Press, 1987.
3. *Pillars of Flame: Power, Priesthood, and Spiritual Maturity.* San Francisco: Harper & Row, 1988.
4. *Seasons of Death and Life: A Wilderness Memoir.* San Francisco: Harper & Row, 1990.

ALEXANDER SCHMEMANN (1890–1983)

Father Alexander was as well known for his sermons broadcast each week to his Russian brethren over Radio Liberty as for his teaching and theological writings at St. Vladimir's Seminary in New York City. He is as fine a representative of the Russian Orthodox tradition as one can find in this century. The great Russian novelist Alexander Solzhenitsyn, who listened to many of Schmemann's talks on the radio, wrote to him in 1972 and said the following: "It amazes me how authentic, contemporary and eloquent the art of [your] preaching is. Not a note of affectation, not a millimeter of stretching the interpretation . . . but always, powerfully profound thought and profound feeling" (Schmemann, 1, 7).

Although Schmemann's writings were not well known outside the Orthodox tradition, Thomas Merton often spoke very highly of his works and his book *For the Life of the World*, which was widely read in ecumenical circles. Schmemann also made available to Western audiences some of the best of Russian Orthodox theology through his book *Ultimate Questions: An Anthology of Russian Religious Thought* (1965).

We have gleaned from the following:

1. *Celebration of Faith.* Crestwood, N.Y.: St. Vladimir's Seminary Press, 1991.
2. *For the Life of the World: Sacraments and Orthodoxy.* New York: St. Vladimir's Seminary Press, 1973. (Also published [in part] as *Sacraments and Orthodoxy* [New York: Herder & Herder, 1965].)

DOROTHEE SOELLE (b. 1929)

Dorothee Soelle, writer and teacher, is well known to contemporary readers of liberation theology, though her work cannot be confined to that category alone. She has inspired many of her students at Union Theological Seminary in New York City and in Hamburg, Germany, during the last twenty-five years.

Her life reflects her theology, as she has brought a postwar generation of Germans to reflect on the relationship between politics and prayer, contemplation and action. Soelle is well known as a leader of the German peace movement. She has always held as a central thesis the notion that a Christian's first and most fundamental response is to the crucified Christ, and that one must consider the implications of that response in and toward those who are "victimized" in our world. Soelle's writings and life merge theology, spirituality, and action. We have gleaned from the following:

1. *Suffering.* Philadelphia: Fortress Press, 1975.
2. *Death by Bread Alone.* Philadelphia: Fortress Press, 1975.

(We call your attention to a recent book in which, through a series of meditations, she introduces the reader to a four-step program of liberation theology: *On Earth as in Heaven: A Liberation Spirituality of Sharing* [Louisville: Westminster John Knox Press, 1993].)

JOSEPH B. SOLOVEITCHIK (1903–1993)

Soloveitchik was born in Russia in 1903. He has been regarded as the leading authority on the meaning of the Jewish law and has been a leader in building bridges between Orthodox Judaism and the modern world. He lived in Boston beginning in 1932 and taught for many years at Yeshiva University in New York City.

His book *The Lonely Man of Faith* shows how joy is mixed with longing in the spiritual life. This mix is born from his European experience and that of the Jews in this century, but it also transcends a time and a people's experience. It reflects what many "spiritual" writings say: that joy and sorrow spring from the same source and are best understood in contexts of love and compassion. We have gleaned from the following:

1. *The Lonely Man of Faith.* Garden City, N.Y.: Doubleday & Co, 1965.
2. *Halakhic Man.* Philadelphia: Jewish Publication Society of America, 1983.

WILLIAM STRINGFELLOW (1928–1985)

William Stringfellow was born on April 26, 1928, in Johnston, Rhode Island. He graduated *cum laude* from Bates College in Lewiston, Maine, in 1949. He then attended the London School of Economics as a research fellow in 1950. He received his LL.B. from Harvard University in 1956.

From 1957 to 1960 he was in private legal practice in East Harlem, New York City. His book about his poverty law work and his life in East Harlem, *My People Is the Enemy* (1964), left no doubt about his devoted and lifelong commitment to issues of social justice and his biblical faith.

In 1970 Stringfellow provided sanctuary for Daniel Berrigan at his Block Island, Rhode Island, home, "The Eschaton." His legal defense work on behalf of peace and justice continued until his untimely death at age fifty-six. He was a member of the Faith and Order Commission of the World Council of Churches and served in many lay leadership roles within the Episcopal Church.

Stringfellow's writings and lecturing throughout the 1960s and 1970s also established him as one of America's most original theologians. When Karl Barth visited the United States in the early 1960s, he called William Stringfellow "the conscientious and thoughtful New York attorney . . . who caught my attention more than any other person (Barth, 4, ix). Once, when asked if he was a "Barthian," Stringfellow replied that he had read very little of Barth and that his theological training consisted largely in reading the Bible and the *New York Times*.

Ill health plagued Stringfellow during much of his life. He lived with pain and grief and discussed these in his books *A Second Birthday* and *A Simplicity of Faith: My Experiences in Mourning* (1982). He died at his Block Island home in March 1985, after a protracted illness; he had just completed his last book, *The Politics of Spirituality* (the principal editor of this book had the honor of editing and working on it with Bill during the last months of his life). Daniel Berrigan said of Bill Stringfellow at his funeral:

> It is to his supreme honor . . . that in his life, the word of God and his own word merged and were one. He kept the word of God so close, so jealously, with such fervor and attention and acute irony and sense of judgment and anger and reverence and fear and so much more—he kept that word in such wise that the word of God and its keeping became his own word and its keeping.
>
> For thousands of us, he became the honored keeper and guardian of the word of God; that is to say, a Christian who could be trusted to keep his word, which was God's word made his own. To keep that word close, to speak it afresh, to make it new.
>
> . . . And that word, which he kept and guarded and cherished—it now keeps him. That is the way with the word, which we name Christ. The covenant keeps us, who keep the covenant.[4]

We have gleaned from the following writings of William Stringfellow:

1. *An Ethic for Christians and Other Aliens in a Strange Land*. Waco, Tex.: Word Books, 1973.
2. *Conscience and Obedience*. Waco, Tex.: Word Books, 1977.

3. *The Politics of Spirituality*. Philadelphia: Westminster Press, 1984.
4. *A Second Birthday*. Garden City, N.Y.: Doubleday & Co., 1970.

(We call your attention to a new book: *A Keeper of the Word: Selected Writings of William Stringfellow*, edited by Bill Wylie Kellerman [Grand Rapids: Wm. B. Eerdmans Publishing Co., 1994]. This book makes difficult-to-find Stringfellow writings easily available to the reading public for the first time.)

PIERRE TEILHARD DE CHARDIN (1881–1955)

Pierre Teilhard de Chardin was born on May 1, 1881. He grew up with a love of the natural world ingrained in him. At eighteen he attained his baccalaureate and entered the Jesuit novitiate at Aix-en-Provence.

From 1905 to 1908, Teilhard taught physics and chemistry in Cairo. After teaching in Egypt, he went to England for his final training as a priest. There he began to see how everything in nature, including human beings, was intricately and spiritually connected.

World War I halted his scientific research. He joined the Eighth Regiment as a stretcher-bearer and was decorated twice. In 1919 he returned to his scientific career. He studied under Marcellin Boule at the Natural History Museum in Paris. In 1923 he left for Tientsin in China to join a French paleontological mission. He stayed for a few weeks and then went into Inner Mongolia and the Ordos desert with Père Emile Licent.

The boldness of Teilhard's theological views got him barred by the church from teaching in Europe, and he returned to China. He later traveled to India and visited America several times. During his return visits to China between 1935 and 1938, he saw the dissolution of the Chinese National Institute that had begun ten years earlier. For six years beginning in 1939, he witnessed the dim atmosphere of a China dominated by the Japanese. During his many sojourns in China, Teilhard wrote his spiritual masterpiece, *The Divine Milieu (Le Milieu divin)*.

In 1951, after he was elected to the French Academy of Sciences, he went to live in New York as a member of the Wenner-Gren Foundation. He returned to Paris briefly in 1954 and died of a stroke in 1955.

We have gleaned from:

1. *Le Milieu divin: An Essay on the Interior Life.* London: Fontana Books, 1964.
2. *Letters from a Traveller.* New York: Harper & Row, Harper Torch-books, 1968.

(Among Teilhard de Chardin's more technical, though also spiritual, writings was the well-known *The Phenomenon of Man* [1959].)

MOTHER TERESA OF CALCUTTA (b. 1910)

She was born Agnes Gonxha Bojaxhiu to Albanian parents in Skopje, Yugoslavia. She attended the government school and became a member of a Catholic sodality. She decided to join the missionary Sisters of Loreto, and in 1928 she was sent to Loreto Abbey at Rathfarnham, Ireland. From there she was sent to India to begin her novitiate in Darjeeling. From 1929 to 1948 she taught geography at St. Mary's High School in Calcutta. She was principal at the school for a few years. In 1931 she took her first vows in Darjeeling, and in 1937 she took her final vows.

On September 10, 1946, now known as "Inspiration Day," Mother Teresa heard a second call of God. In August 1948 she laid aside her Loreto habit and clothed herself in a white sari with a blue border across the shoulder. From that point her story is well known, as she formed the Missionaries of Charity in 1950 and began work in the Calcutta slums with "the poorest of the poor." The new congregation was approved and instituted in Calcutta and soon spread throughout India.

In 1965 the Missionaries of Charity became a Society of Pontifical Right. In July the Venezuela center was opened by Mother Teresa near Caracas. In December 1967 she opened a center in Sri Lanka near Colombo; another center was opened in the slums of Rome in 1968. Soon centers were to open around the world: in Australia; Jordan; Belfast, Northern Ireland; New York City; the Gaza strip; Lima, Peru; Yemen; and Bangladesh.

Now an Indian citizen, Mother Teresa was awarded the Jawaharlal Nehru Award for International Understanding by the Indian government in 1969. In 1971 she was awarded the Pope John XXIII Peace Prize by Pope Paul VI. Many prizes were to follow, including the Templeton Prize in Religion.

We have gleaned from:

1. *The Love of Christ: Spiritual Counsels.* Edited by Georges Gorrée and Jean Barbier. San Francisco: Harper & Row, 1982.
2. *A Gift for God: Prayers and Meditations.* San Francisco: Harper & Row, 1975.

(Please also note the two books cited in the references for Brother Roger of Taizé, which Mother Teresa coauthored with Brother Roger.)

EVELYN UNDERHILL (1875–1941)

An English poet, novelist, and writer on mysticism, Evelyn was the daughter of Sir Arthur Underhill. She was educated at King's College for Women in London, of which she was made an honorary fellow in 1913 and a fellow in 1927.

From 1900 to 1920 she composed light verse and novels. She was Upton Lecturer on the Philosophy of Religion at Manchester College, Oxford, in 1921. Aberdeen University conferred on her an honorary doctor of divinity degree in 1939.

Her book *Mysticism* was published in 1911 and went through many editions. In 1926 she published *Concerning the Inner Life. Consciousness* (1930) became as popular as *Mysticism.*

The overall influence of Underhill's writings on mysticism and the inner life should not be underestimated. They have been a foundation stone for much research in this century and have inspired many of the authors who are anthologized in this volume. We have gleaned from:

1. *An Anthology of the Love of God: From the Writings of Evelyn Underhill.* Edited by Lumsden Barkway. New York: David McKay Co., 1953.
2. *Practical Mysticism.* New York: E. P. Dutton & Co., 1915.

SIMONE WEIL (1909–1943)

André Gide called Simone Weil the most spiritual writer of the twentieth century. Her writings are varied and often difficult to penetrate but always deeply rewarding. She was widely read in political philosophy, classical literature, Greek philosophy, and the religious literature of Christianity, Hinduism, and Buddhism. Her activism for the poor began when she was a young child during World War I: she refused to eat sugar because the soldiers at the front were unable to have it; she also refused to wear warm socks because the poor children of workers were unable to have them.

Weil received her baccalaureate with distinction at the age of fifteen and went on to study under the well-known philosopher and essayist Alain. In 1931 she received a graduate degree from the Sorbonne and was appointed to the secondary school for girls at Le Puy. While in Le Puy, she contributed to the review *La Révolution Prolétarienne,* walked in picket lines, and refused to eat more than the unemployed workers were able to eat who were on relief. She also taught courses on the classical Greek tragedies to miners.

She took a year's leave in 1934 to work in the Renault automobile factory to experience the life of a working person. Despite severe migraine headaches, she rejected any type of comfort that might make her different from the other workers. In 1936 she traveled to Barcelona to share in the suffering that the Republican army was going through in the Spanish Civil War. An injury behind the lines forced her return to France.

In 1937–38 Simone Weil experienced several "mystical" experiences: one in a small peasant village in Portugal; one in the chapel of Saint Francis in Assisi; and another at the Abbey of Solesmes in France. Her writings from that point took a more spiritual turn, though she continued to address issues of oppression, injustice, and human suffering. In 1940, when Paris was occupied by the Germans, Weil's Jewish family background forced her and her family to go to Marseilles and try to leave France. There she immersed herself in agricultural work, studied Greek and Hindu philosophy, had conversations with Lanza del Vasto, and was influenced deeply by the Catholic priest Father Perrin.

In May 1942 Weil went with her parents to America. She soon returned to England, where she worked for the Free French Resistance. Some of her best spiritual and political writings were written during her short period in London. She was weak with tuberculosis but refused to eat any more than the rations allowed to her compatriots in France. She died of voluntary starvation on August 24, 1943, at age thirty-four.

Our gleanings come from a variety of sources.

1. *First and Last Notebooks.* Translated by Richard Rees. London: Oxford University Press, 1970.
2. *Gravity and Grace.* Translated by Emma Craufurd. London: Routledge & Kegan Paul, 1972.
3. *The Iliad, or The Poem of Force.* Translated by Mary McCarthy, Wallingford. Pa.: Pendle Hill Pamphlet 91, 1981.
4. *Oppression and Liberty.* Translated by Arthur Wills and John Petrie. Amherst, Mass.: University of Massachusetts Press, 1973.
5. *Science, Necessity and the Love of God.* Translated by Richard Rees. London: Oxford University Press, 1968.
6. "Human Personality." In *Two Moral Essays.* Translated by Richard Rees. Wallingford, Pa.: Pendle Hill Pamphlet 240, 1981.
7. *Waiting for God.* Translated by Emma Craufurd. New York: Harper & Row, Colophon Books, 1951.

(We also refer readers to an important work of Simone Weil from which we have not gleaned: *The Need for Roots* [1971]. Also helpful are the biography by David McLellan, *Simone Weil, Utopian Pessimist* (1989); and a volume of essays edited by the author: Richard H. Bell, ed., *Simone Weil's Philosophy of Culture* [Cambridge: Cambridge University Press, 1993].)

Notes

INTRODUCTION

1. Ruth was a Moabite who came to Bethlehem and gleaned in the fields of Boaz, who was of Elimelech's family. Her faithfulness gave her a place in the family of faith, as Matthew recounts in his lineage of Jesus (Matt. 1:1–16).

2. In this Introduction, we will note only those quotations that are not already among the gleanings. The references for those appearing among the gleanings, such as this one, are specifically identified in that section.

3. William Stringfellow, *The Politics of Spirituality* (Philadelphia: Westminster Press, 1984), 19. We are further warned by Stringfellow of some of the particular pitfalls that he experienced within the American religious scene, especially with regard to clergy use of the term: " 'Spirituality' is for many, particularly church folk, an intimidating term. It is recited authoritatively, yet merely conceals a void. At the same time, it is rarely challenged in practice by listeners because they do not want to be considered obtuse 'spiritually.' " The term has many of the same deceptive characteristics as "professional" and "political" jargon do. Stringfellow concludes: "The common practice of resorting to such terms as spirituality in order to hide ignorance or mask incoherence or disguise a voice immeasurably increases and complicates the inherent vagueness of the language of spirituality" (16).

4. These are discussed at length as "disciplines of the human spirit" in chapters 7 through 10 of Richard H. Bell, *Sensing the Spirit* (Philadelphia: Westminster Press, 1984).

5. The metaphor of "descending image" is developed by Pavel Florensky in his essay "On the Icon," *Eastern Church Review* 8, no. 1 (1976): 33–34.

6. Kathleen Norris, *Dakota: A Spiritual Geography* (New York: Ticknor & Fields, 1993), 23.

7. Ibid., 19.

8. Ibid., 129.

9. Carol Ochs, *Women and Spirituality* (Totowa, N.J.: Rowman & Allanheld, 1983), 141.

10. Ibid., 2.

11. Ibid., 144.

12. Ibid., 138.

13. It was, of course, more than timid actions from people like Havel that brought about the velvet revolution in Czechoslovakia in 1989. The power of this form of spirituality, born in the crucible of the twentieth century, cannot be denied. Havel's life is witness to how spirituality can be geopolitically transforming as well as personally transforming.

14. Herbert Fingarette, *Confucius: The Secular as the Sacred* (New York: Harper & Row, Harper Torchbooks, 1972), 60. Fingarette, in his fine book, discusses how this idea is central in the philosophy of Confucius and that we in the "Western world" could learn from this Chinese spiritual tradition. Taoism, too, has a strong sense of community and has appeal for a natural spirituality.

GLEANINGS

1. To be published in a forthcoming volume of *The Way of Silent Love.*

2. This "Letter from Warsaw" was addressed to thousands of young people gathered for a meeting in London in December 1981; it was a sign of hope and reconciliation from an Eastern Europe that was struggling for freedom.

3. This line is known as the Jesus Prayer, or the Prayer of the Heart. It is used in meditation and contemplative prayer, especially in the Eastern Orthodox traditions. It is often shortened to simply "Lord Jesus Christ, have mercy on me, a sinner."

4. *Tzimtzum* (or *Tsim Tsum*) is a concept associated with the Jewish mystical tradition of Isaac Luria (1534–1572) and the Cabala. It was the notion that God contracted or withdrew into God's self in order to leave a creation that could then establish a relationship with God. By *Tzimtzum* God and the world could retain their own being at creation.

5. Yuri Gagarin was the first Russian cosmonaut to orbit the Earth.

APPENDIX A

1. Parker Palmer, *The Active Life: A Spirituality of Work, Creativity, and Caring* (San Francisco: Harper & Row, 1990), 18.

2. Quoted in Matthew Fox, *Meditations with Meister Eckhart* (Santa Fe, N. Mex.: Bear & Co., 1983), 15.

3. Ibid., 120.

APPENDIX B

1. This is a line from Stephen Spender's poem "I Think Continually of Those Who Are Truly Great," in his *Collected Poems 1928–1985* (New York: Random House), 1986, 30.

2. Material in this sketch is revised from *The Westminster Dictionary of Christian Spirituality*, ed. Gordon S. Wakefield (Philadelphia: Westminster Press, 1983).

3. As found in *The Words of Martin Luther King Jr.*, selected and introduced by Coretta Scott King (New York: Newmarket Press, 1987), 95.

4. Daniel Berrigan, "Keeper of the Word: To Celebrate the Death and Life of William Stringfellow," *Sojourners* (May 1985): 33.

A Short Selection of General Books on Spirituality

This list includes mostly current, nontechnical works on the nature and practice of spirituality. Some are themselves "spiritual writings" like those from which we have gleaned: for example, the works of Quaker writers Thomas R. Kelley and Douglas V. Steere, both of whom perhaps should have selections among the gleanings.

Bell, Richard H. *Sensing the Spirit*. Philadelphia: Westminster Press, 1984.

Bolshakoff, Sergius, and M. Basil Pennington, O.C.S.O. *In Search of True Wisdom: Visits to Eastern Spiritual Fathers*. New York: Alba House, 1991. (This is an unusual collection of conversations with Russian Orthodox spiritual writers of the twentieth century who, while in exile from the Communist regime from 1919 through 1990, carried forward the tradition of Orthodox spirituality into Western contexts.)

Brueggemann, Walter. *Praying the Psalms*. Winona, Minn.: Saint Mary's Press, Christian Brothers Publications, 1986.

Edwards, Tilden. *Living in the Presence: Disciplines for the Spiritual Heart*. San Francisco: Harper & Row, 1987.

———. *Living with Apocalypse: Spiritual Resources for Social Compassion*. New York: Harper & Row, 1984.

Gausseron, Nicole. *The Little Notebook: The Journal of a Contemporary Woman's Encounters with Jesus*. Translated and edited by William Skudlarek and Hilary Thimmesh. San Francisco: Harper, 1995.

Jones, Alan. *Soulmaking*. San Francisco: Harper & Row, 1985.

Jones, W. Paul. *Trumpet at Full Moon: An Introduction to Christian Spirituality as Diverse Practice*. Louisville: Westminster John Knox Press, 1992.

Kelley, Thomas R. *A Testament of Devotion*. New York: Harper & Brothers, 1941.

Kelsey, Morton. *Companions on the Inner Way: The Art of Spiritual Guidance*. New York: Crossroad, 1983.

———. *The Other Side of Silence: A Guide to Christian Meditation*. New York: Paulist Press, 1976.

Kornfield, Jack. *A Path with a Heart*. New York: Bantam Books, 1993.

Leech, Kenneth. *Experiencing God: Theology as Spirituality*. San Francisco: Harper & Row, 1985.

————. *The Eye of the Storm: Living Spiritually in the Real World*. San Francisco: Harper & Row, 1992.

McGinnis, James. *Journey into Compassion: A Spirituality for the Long Haul*. Bloomington, Ind.: Meyer-Stone Books and the Institute for Peace and Justice, St. Louis, Mo., 1989. (A new edition is being published by Orbis Books [1994].)

McManus, Jim, C.S.S.R. *The Healing Power of the Sacraments*. Notre Dame, Ind.: Ave Maria Press, 1984.

May, Gerald. *The Awakened Heart*. San Francisco: Harper & Row, 1991.

Nielsen, H. A. *The Bible—As If for the First Time*. Philadelphia: Westminster Press, 1984.

Palmer, Parker. *The Active Life: A Spirituality of Work, Creativity, and Caring*. San Francisco: Harper & Row, 1990.

Rice, Howard L. *Reformed Spirituality: An Introduction for Believers*. Louisville, Ky.: Westminster John Knox Press, 1991.

Saliers, Don E. *Worship and Spirituality*. Philadelphia: Westminster Press, 1984.

Skudlarek, William, O.S.B., ed. *The Continuing Quest for God: Monastic Spirituality in Tradition and Transition*. Collegeville, Minn.: Liturgical Press, 1982.

Steere, Douglas V. *On Beginning from Within*. New York: Harper & Brothers, 1943.

————. *Gleanings: A Random Harvest*. Nashville: Upper Room, 1986.

————. *On Listening to Another*. New York: Harper & Brothers, 1955.

————. *Prayer and Worship*. New York: Association Press, 1938.

Wakefield, Gordon S., ed. *The Westminster Dictionary of Christian Spirituality*. Philadelphia: Westminster Press, 1983.

Williams, Rowan. *The Wound of Knowledge: Christian Spirituality from the New Testament to St. John of the Cross*. London: Darton, Longman & Todd, 1979.

Entrepreneuring: The Ten Commandments for Building a Growth Company
by
Steven C. Brandt

Published by:
Archipelago Publishing
P.O. Box 1249
Friday Harbor, WA 98250
(800) 360-6166 Fax: 360-378-7097
info@gmex.com
http://www.gmex.com

Library of Congress Catalog Card Number: 96-85780

ISBN 1-888925-02-7

Book Design & Layout by Art Design/Bruce Conway,
Friday Harbor, WA
Printed in the U.S.A.

What professionals are saying about...

Entrepreneuring: The Ten Commandments for Building a Growth Company
by
Steven C. Brandt

"Vintage Brandt: Clear, concise, and written with experience. A great business idea plus this book will go a long way toward building a business success story."
 - *Henry L. B. Wilder, Dougery & Wilder–Venture Capital (San Francisco)*

"Sophisticated ideas made readable and usable.The author obviously speaks from experience."
 - *Robert K. Jaedicke, former Dean, Stanford Graduate School of Business*

"Succinct, practical, excellent cases. A valuable combination of real world experience, academic discipline, and humor–which is rare."
 - *Freeman Ford, CEO & Founder, FAFCO (NASDAQ)*

"A primer for entrepreneurs. I wish I had read this book years ago; it would have saved me a lot of trouble!"
 - *Bob Hannah, Founder, R.S. Hannah Co.*

"Remarkably helpful. High tech, low tech, or no tech, a must read."
 - *Forbes Powell, President, Luxel, Inc. (former VP, TRW)*

"In business, going into business, thinking of business? Read this book."
 - *Bill Briner, President, Tahoe Maritime Museum*

"Comprehensive and to the point. I recommend it to everyone who comes to me for help in building a business."
 - *Mike Irvin, CPA, Irvin & Abrahamson (Silicon Valley)*

"An important road map for starting a business. These ten commandments are central to an entrepreneur's bible."
 - *Robert Tufts, Corp. Attorney, Petty, Andrews, & Tufts (Silicon Valley)*

"Solid material. We are including it in our courses as a practical guide to building a business."
 - *K.R. Smith, President, Altos Education Network*

If you want to build a business, here is your handbook.